RIDING THE CREATIVE ROLLERCOASTER

D0143912

RIDING THE CREATIVE ROLLERCOASTER

HOW LEADERS EVOKE CREATIVITY, PRODUCTIVITY AND INNOVATION

DR NICK UDALL

KoganPage

LONDON PHILADELPHIA NEW DELHI

First published in Great Britain and the United States in 2014 by Kogan Page Limited

2nd Floor, 45 Gee Street	1518 Walnut Street, Suite 1100	4737/23 Ansari Road
London EC1V 3RS	Philadelphia PA 19102	Daryaganj
United Kingdom	USA	New Delhi 110002
www.koganpage.com		India

© Nick Udall, 2014

ISBN   978 0 7494 7213 9
E-ISBN   978 0 7494 7214 6

British Library Cataloguing-in-Publication Data

A CIP record for this book is available from the British Library.

CIP data is available
Library of Congress Control Number: 2012046241

Typeset by Graphicraft Limited, Hong Kong
Print production managed by Jellyfish
Printed and bound in Great Britain by CPI Group (UK) Ltd, Croydon CR0 4YY

Dedicated to Caroline, Kaia and Zen.

CONTENTS

LIST OF FIGURES

LIST OF TABLES

ACKNOWLEDGEMENTS

I feel enormously lucky. I have so many wonderful people around me that support me, challenge me, and co-create with me.

I need to start by acknowledging and thanking my family who resource me to be able to walk a purposeful path. Their love, warmth and generosity inspire me daily. I especially need to mention my beautiful wife, Caroline, and my gorgeous kids Kaia and Zen, who are all my inspiration.

I also need to appreciate my second family, the **nowhere** community. I am only able to write and share the thoughts and experiences in this book because of them and our ongoing communal adventure. I feel blessed to be working alongside such an extraordinary bunch of misfits.

I would like to appreciate the World Economic Forum, and my fellow members of the Global Agenda Council on New Models of Leadership, for their passion and insight into why new forms of leadership are needed more than ever before.

I would also like to thank Jo Howard for her support and guidance over many, many years, and ultimately for hooking me up with Kogan Page; and Matthew Smith at Kogan Page for taking on this project and bringing his own passion and creativity to the party.

Lastly, I want to thank all of the leaders that I have had the privilege of meeting and working with. Leadership can be a lonely endeavour and I feel deeply appreciative of their willingness to share their candid musings, reflections and experiences.

HYPOTHESIS

INNOVATION EMERGES FROM A CO-CREATIVE FREQUENCY, NOT A PROCESS

Innovation emerges from a co-creative frequency, not a process. The way we think, relate, learn and organize either moves us towards this frequency or away from it. The leadership challenge of our time is to evoke 'the music of innovation' – to tune the frequency at which our teams and organizations operate – by design.

THE MUSIC OF INNOVATION

I remember sitting one day in a hotel restaurant, after lunch, with a senior leader from one of our clients. We had just completed a two-day deep-dive with the top 20 or so leaders of a global corporation helping them to develop the core energy needed to launch into an organization-wide transformation. It had all gone very well, and as normal I was particularly relieved.

I was very fond of this leader. He was a year or two away from retirement. He loved what he did and had become a wise old owl.

As often happens, the conversation, post creative intervention, drifted into how we create the conditions for creative insight and collective breakthrough to emerge. After a few minutes of me trying my best to explain how our practice works, he looked at me and said, 'What you mean to say is that you are helping us evoke the "music of innovation"'. I was immediately struck by the synchronicity of his metaphor. I had recently begun to explain that cultures of innovation operate as a certain frequency, yet I hadn't taken the thought as far as he had in that moment. I loved it, and have played with this notion ever since.

A PASSION FOR THE FUTURE OF LEADERSHIP

I've always been passionate about creativity and innovation. I've known this since I was a kid. More recently, though, another passion has crept up on me, a passion for the future of leadership.

Since the age of 23 I've been working with CEOs and the executive teams of major corporations. And, for the last 15 years I've been the CEO of **nowhere**, leading a specialist community of creative-catalysts who work with executive leaders to build cultures of innovation and develop breakthrough strategies through the power of creative teams and evocative leadership. Our primary driver has been, and continues to be, to release the co-creative potential of teams and organizations.

I have therefore had the privilege of working with amazing leaders and teams all over the world. Over this time the need for innovation within all industries, and at all levels, has continued to grow; and, the world has become a more complex, interdependent and volatile place.

I've also noticed how more and more leaders are hitting up against a glass ceiling where their honed performance and delivery skills are becoming less and less effective at driving the level and rate of innovation that is needed now.

Unfortunately we (society as a whole) are all the poorer because of this.

To this effect, I have become very interested in the question: What are the new and next generation of leadership skills we now need to call forward into the world?

In 2011 I was invited to be one of the founding members of the World Economic Forum's Global Agenda Council on New Models of Leadership, with pioneers like Dan Goleman (author of *Emotional Intelligence*, 1996) and Otto Scharmer (author of *Theory U*, 2009). I went through my usual fears of whether I could contribute. Did I really have anything useful, let alone new, to say?

Over time something started to show itself, first taking form as my contribution to a white paper, then as an evocative talk, and finally a short book – this book!

What emerged was the naming of a leadership threshold. From my experience, those leaders that have learned to step over this threshold (temporarily or permanently) are able to open up a whole new world of conscious, creative and commercial possibilities. What was previously hidden, invisible and unavailable becomes available to them.

These leaders create and shape futures we all want to move towards. They disturb the present in order to allow the new to emerge. And, they create containers and hold spaces in which teams, functions, organizations, and even ecosystems of organizations, regularly experience moments of creative insight and collective breakthrough – the true source of product, service, process, go-to-market, business model, strategy and cultural innovation.

These containers and spaces are needed now more than ever before in business, in education, in health and in government; for if we are to shape more purposeful, productive and sustainable futures, fit for generations to come, we have to innovate our way there.

And, in order to generate innovation across such a breadth and depth of organizations and institutions, and at an increased rate, we need to develop leaders who can catalyse creative insight and collective breakthrough, not by accident, but by design.

THE MAGIC TRIUMVIRATE: INNOVATION, CREATIVITY AND CONSCIOUSNESS

To do this, more leaders need to understand how innovation is an output of our creativity, and how creativity is an outcome of our level of consciousness.

I call this interplay between innovation, creativity and consciousness, the magic triumvirate.

At its essence, innovation is about successfully bringing 'the new' to the world – 'successfully' being the operative word. In a business context, successful refers to the commercialization (scaling and replicating) of 'the new'. In a research context, it refers to the acceptance and application of 'the new' by wider peer groups. In a social context, successful innovations are measured through impact, progress and/or sustainability.

So if innovation is about bringing the new to the world, then creativity is about bringing 'the new' to mind. And, let's here and now dispel the myth that creativity is about idea generation, brainstorming, poetry, or even the Arts in general. They are all outcomes or outputs of creative processes, but they are not creativity.

Creativity is the dance between what we know and what we don't know, and it is through this dance that we make meaning of the world around us, making the unknown knowable, the unconscious conscious, and the invisible visible. This dance is fundamental to the emergence of newness (new to me and/or new to the world) in all disciplines. Yet we've never worked out how to teach it in schools or to actively develop it in organizations.

Moreover, there is an art to actively bringing the new to mind, for our everyday, ego-consciousness hates to be out of control, preferring to keep us within the comfort zone of what we already know. The problem with this is that we then flat-line through life, doing what we've always done.

The challenge is to awaken particular states and qualities of mind that help our creativity flourish, and to interrupt those states of qualities of mind that kill our creativity. To do this we need to first raise our level of self, relational and systemic awareness; and then tap into a wider collective intelligence.

COLLECTIVE CREATIVITY AND COLLECTIVE CONSCIOUSNESS (OR MIND)

It is widely acknowledged that innovation, bringing the new into the world, is more often than not a collective endeavour. It requires a great deal of effort by a focused group, network or community of people. Taking a new molecule to market, a new play to the stage, a new seed to the farmer's field, or bringing any other new product, service or platform into the world, takes time and requires resource.

Creativity on the other hand is more regularly seen as an individual activity. This assumption is embedded in the statement, 'I'm not very creative', which I hear often from people.

Innovation

Bringing the new to the world

Creativity

Bringing the new to mind

Consciousness

States and qualities of mind

FIGURE 1.1 The magic triumvirate

I believe we are all inherently creative. Unfortunately many of us have had our creativity educated out of us. We are then socially conditioned to develop various mental and emotional filters (including the fear of failure), to maintain the status quo and keep us fearful of, and even blind to, what we don't know.

Over time these filters make us more reliant on the shorter dendrite branches in the left hemisphere of our brains, the part that drives our rational and analytical responses; rather than the longer and broader dendrite structures in the right hemisphere of our brains which resource other, more indirect ways of knowing. This bias to our shorter, more ordered neural networks, decreases our ability to make the new and novel connections essential for forming new thoughts and generating new insights.

To access the more chaotic, meandering pathways of our right hemispheres, we need to step more regularly and more profoundly into the unknown. Then and only then can we truly value difference, play with new and novel intersections and lean into the void – the empty, co-creative spaces that lie between now and then, this and that, today and tomorrow, and you and me. For it is from these empty spaces that the future emerges.

But this isn't just an individual phenomenon.

A group or community can also access a wider collective intelligence. Rather like the neural networks of our brains, they can learn to tap into the new and novel intersections that lie in the space between them.

For example, teams naturally begin by using the equivalent of their left hemisphere, sharing and working with what they already know – the facts, assumptions, habits and beliefs. But, if they stay with it, and are able to move to the edges of what they know, a team can tap into the equivalent of their right

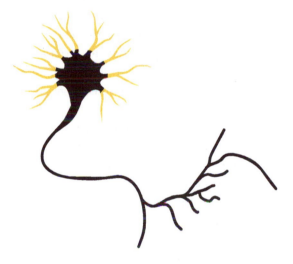

FIGURE 1.2 Short vs long dendrites

hemisphere. They learn to slow down, surrender to not-knowing, wander with wonder, see pattern, play with rhythm and find and follow flow.

Of course, the more people, the greater the number of potential new and novel intersections, and the increased likelihood of creating, shaping and making new associations. However, for this to happen we need to create containers and hold spaces that tune the collective to the same co-creative frequency. Then teams, groups and organizations can co-creatively meet the world around them, start to work co-creatively with each other, and thereby open themselves to more regular and more profound moments of creative insight and collective breakthrough. This is where what they communally know suddenly reorders to a higher level of collective and creative consciousness.

This is why I view teams, communities and organizations as conscious organisms. They have collective awareness (and blindness). They have their own sense of subjectivity ie their way of making meaning of the world. They have common emotions and moods. They feel enlivened and awake, or tired and asleep. And they have their own executive control systems. Therefore I believe we need to call forward a new and next generation of subtle leadership skills that can tune groups and collectives to frequencies that expand their everyday consciousness. Catalysing these frequencies is key to releasing the co-creative potential of teams and of organizations, for generating and accelerating innovation, and for shaping futures we all want to move towards.

Think Talk Hold space

FIGURE 1.3 Three keys

THE THREE KEYS: THINKING, TALKING AND HOLDING SPACE

It is also important to go back to the essence of executive leadership. In essence, executive leaders only really do three things. They *think*. They *talk*. And they *hold space*. Let me explain.

I remember being told a story. I'm sure there are many versions of this story out there.

One day the nine-year-old daughter of an executive leader asked her father, 'What do you do all day?'

Her father responded by saying, 'I run the supply chain for a high street retailer.'

His daughter looked at him blankly and then said, 'I don't understand. So what do you actually do all day?'

'I make sure that we get the right products in the right stores at the right time.'

'Yeah, but what do YOU do all day?'

Her father stopped, realizing he wasn't answering her question well enough.

Then, surprising himself, he said, 'What I do is think and talk. I sit in meetings and talk to people. I sit on my own and think how I can do things better. And together we try to figure out how we can make our company more successful.'

We often take thinking and talking for granted, as if the way we think and talk (including the ways in which we communicate in person, and through a myriad of media) is the only way we can think and talk. This is just not so.

The challenge for leaders is to learn how to think differently, and even more powerfully, how to think differently together.

Similarly, how we talk is often a less elegant expression of how we think. It is easy to get stuck in conversations that are nothing more than the ping-pong of opinions, as opposed to the co-creation of new thought and the shaping of new meaning.

The irony is how much time, energy and ultimately money is wasted when leaders get together (in meetings) where, without knowing it, they get stuck arguing for their own limitations.

I recently catalysed a meeting of 13 CEOs, each of them very successful businessmen in their own right, with huge experience. Over three days this group of opinionated, self-assured leaders (as they would have described themselves) were exposed to new ways of working where they learned to slow down and weave their wisdom together. By the middle of the second day they started catching glimpses of what it meant to literally think together. They experienced moments of optimal flow.

They also noticed how they entered conversations – their intent, words and tone – either enabled or disabled the likelihood of this collective phenomenon. So how they were – in their being – made all the difference.

What emerged from this experiment, of tapping into the co-creative space between them, were wholly new business opportunities. They discovered that their habitual ways of thinking (that had got them to where they are today) were also full of self-limiting beliefs and assumptions. They were held in a space where it was now in their power to enquire into and challenge their own belief systems. The world, and their interpretation of it, was no longer static and objective; it was now fluid and subjective. They'd touched into a co-creative realm that they never knew existed.

How we think and how we talk are art forms in their own right. Through exposure and practice we can discover new dimensions to both. Transforming how we think and talk is part of developing what we call *evocative leadership*.

However, before I move on, let me clarify that leaders at all levels are more than how they think, talk and hold space. Whether they are generalists or specialists (with a clear vocation, expertise and/or craft), leaders have a complex array of challenges thrust upon them. And many, many books have been written about this.

One of the most important leadership challenges is to make tough decisions in light of different choices, trade-offs and dilemmas, all in service of navigating teams and organizations towards greater 'success'. Yet one could argue that some of the best decisions they could make are still out of their current awareness. And yet leaders still need to make decisions.

Moreover the vast majority of leaders make decisions based on the assimilation of the best available 'facts' (often a judgement on the past), and by using the power of their intellects. My argument, is that this is no longer enough.

So we then come to how leaders affect 'space'. All leaders affect space whether they know it or not. By default of their structural position in a hierarchy, and/or by their intellectual capability, their charisma, or their presence, leaders determine the quality and quantity of space available in their organizations. The danger is that leaders fill the space themselves rather than describe and hold spaces in which people and teams can step in, make meaning, play with possibilities and allow the new to emerge. The nature of the available space, and the leader's role within it, defines boundaries, and, in turn, determines the level of productivity and creativity in an organizational system.

A team meeting, a town hall gathering, a new vision or strategy, or just how a leader is in their being, are all opportunities and interventions that either create and open spaces for the new to emerge or that close them down. The challenge, in the context of innovation, is to create spaces that feel held, purposeful and charged with energy, and that call people forward to do things they never thought they could do. These spaces allow new possibilities to arise and latent potential to

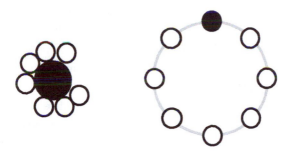

FIGURE 1.4 Taking up space vs holding space

be released. And, this is before a thought is thought, or a word is spoken.

The challenge is that many leaders are good at, taught to, and rewarded for, taking up space, as opposed to the art of creating and holding space.

If we are lucky it's their strengths (vision, breadth and depth of capability, speed of thought, etc) that take up the space. If we are unlucky it is their ego, their voice and their inadequacies that take up the space.

The leader may be tapping into their own brilliance, and if they are lucky tapping into the brilliance of some of the people in the wider system. What they won't be doing is tapping into the collective intelligence of the whole. This results in workman-like interactions and transactional exchanges, where people are clear about their tasks, yet unable to tap into their own and each other's magic.

This brings us to the main stage of executive leadership (in fact most levels of leadership) – the meeting. How a leader runs meetings is a critical indicator of their capacity to hold co-creative space and therefore of their level of consciousness.

For example, let me briefly describe two polarities. Many leaders are fanatical about having ordered and orderly meetings. They start with precise and certain agendas, largely filled with routine updates, with limited space for discussion and exploration of the key issues. Their meetings often run late, become ragged, and end with some degree of uncertainty around key decisions, if any decisions are made at all. At the other end of the spectrum are meetings that are designed to embrace and explore both the known and the unknown, allowing new order to emerge over time from the space between.

Leaders can also get stuck in wider organizational meeting patterns, ie this is the way we run meetings around here.

Unfortunately, most organizations have meeting habits that are one-dimensional too – focused solely on driving activity. This is why holding spaces to activate the collective creativity of groups is so important. Together with thinking and talking, these three, simple, and mostly intangible, things are the tools of executive leadership.

Great leadership is a movement from taking up space to beautifully holding space, spaces that use collective intelligence, creative tension and flow to significantly increase productivity and creativity, and thereby the capacity to out-innovate the competition.

The challenge is to move beyond an industrialized view of leadership and innovation as the management of people, processes and resources; to instead see how innovation emerges from co-creative frequencies, generated from containers, spaces and working practices that leverage talent, harness new and novel intersections and release the co-creative potential that lies in the space between.

These containers, spaces and working practices need to be strong enough to hold the uncertainty and emotion that emerges when we disrupt the status quo. They need to be safe enough to speak the truth. They must create the openness and trust needed to step into the unknown. They need to be subtle and still enough to catch glimpses of 'the new'. And they need to be skilful enough to transform creative sparks into innovations.

Creative insight and collective breakthrough are born from the frequencies created in these containers and spaces, and our ability to innovate is dependent upon them. This is how the new comes into the world. And this is how breakthrough happens, not by accident, but by design.

Difference   **+**   Intersection

=

FIGURE 1.5 The secret sauce – working with collective intelligence

✚ Creative Tension ✚ Collective Intelligence

Creative Insight
& Collective
Breakthrough

FIGURE 1.5 Continued

LEANING INTO THE EMERGING FUTURE

Meanwhile, the game is also changing and the implications for leaders are immense. Take your pick: from the impact of hyper-dependency, to the constant introduction of game-changing technologies; from the growing influence of Generation Y and digital natives, to the increase in scarcity on so many fronts; from the complexity of geo-politics, to the fragility of our monetary systems; from the omnipresence of trans-media, to the impact of the well-being economy...

From a creative and innovative point of view, the tensions and chaos that these, and many other factors, are generating are actually good news. From other perspectives these factors can of course be seen as threatening and overwhelming.

For good or ill, 'the new' is always born from the void of uncertainty, and can only ever be understood in hindsight. This is why we need to break free of our obsession with our intellects and our 'need to know'.

Within this dynamic context leadership is no longer just about moving from A (current reality) to B (some future state, point, or goal). B can sometimes be out of date as soon as we start aiming for it, and A is often understood differently by every stakeholder. In a world that is changing so rapidly, pursuing a strategy based on a set of cause-and-effect relationships ignores the reality of the range of unknown factors that will likely emerge and have significant impact on the plan. Linear cause and effect is now only one way of looking at and navigating our increasingly complex and interdependent world. To be clear, having a North Star to aim at, to help us stay on course, can be critical. But, it is just as important to be able to work with emergence, iteration and adaptation.

We have much to celebrate about the power of human intelligence but it is only a part of the equation, especially when it comes to creativity. Our intellects can only take us so far. At some point we need to move beyond it and learn how to work with other forms of knowing.

Creativity is a perfect example, for it incorporates our intellectual capacity, and at the same time is more than that. Born from the dance between the known and the unknown, and between our conscious and our unconscious, creativity requires us to call upon our thoughts, feelings, intuitions and embodied knowing. And yet culturally, when faced with a challenge, we are completely skewed to filling ourselves up with more factual knowledge. And to be fair, when did we get taught how to step into the unknown and to work with the possibilities that arise from not knowing?

Crazy as it may sound, 'not knowing' is a high skill. Holding spaces for something new, especially something new that reorders knowledge that came before, is bloody tricky. This is because we too quickly and too easily self-select data that reinforces what we already know, or just slightly extends what we already know. Very rarely do we let in information that challenges our belief systems or requires our worldviews to bend and flex.

SUMMARY

This book is therefore about:

- Naming a critical leadership, team and organizational threshold, revealing what lies on the other side, and what it takes to step over it.

- Working with innovation, creativity and consciousness as co-creative frequencies.

- The subtle skills needed for creating containers and holding spaces for creative insight and collective breakthrough to emerge.

- Those states and qualities of mind that help our creativity flourish.

- How leaders can very practically lean into the void and learn other ways of knowing that evoke the music of innovation, by design.

Before we jump in, let me also set some other expectations.

I wanted this to be a short book. I can't promise an easy read, but I've tried not to waffle.

I've also never been a fan of case studies as they tend to point to perceived 'best' practice rather than innovative practice. It's great to see and learn what others have done, but I am more interested in the creative challenge of what hasn't been done.

I have tried to be uncompromising on language. I remember 15 years ago being challenged not to use 'consultant speak' when I was trying to help clients see something new. Interestingly, I now see a lot of 'corporate speak' – decks and decks of PowerPoint slides that just make no sense, that go around in circles, and/or that shy away from talking straight. It has become one of those bizarre phenomena of current corporate life.

I've come to realize how important language is to leadership and innovation. I will do my best not to speak or to write oddly. However, I do intend to play with language and with meaning, the reasons for which will become clear as you read further.

Where I can, I will also pepper the landscape that I draw with stories. I am a big believer in the power of story and storytelling, and I hope to use this form at appropriate places and junctures.

This book is not intended as a 'how to' book. All I am able to do through the written word is to outline a critical threshold and point to what lies on the other side. Ultimately, learning the subtle skills and working practices needed to evoke the music of innovation is a journey of first exposure, then experience, practice and mastery. As I will describe later in the book, the challenge is how to develop these subtle skills in months rather than years.

Finally, my invitation to the reader is to slow down, to lean back, and to let something new in. It is from this place, and only from this place, that we can first see, then meet, and eventually step over this subtle leadership threshold. This threshold is a doorway to a new realm, what I will later describe as the *fourth realm*.

In this realm, wondrous things begin to happen out of nowhere. In this realm, we learn to step into the unknown, harness the power of the present moment, see and work with the invisible, and design and catalyse creative insight and collective breakthrough.

This is the realm of collective intelligence. It is where new order emerges from chaos, new pattern emerges from complexity, and innovative foregrounds emerge from strategic backgrounds.

This is where the world that we thought we knew, changes forever.

DESIGNING TRANSFORMATION

I originally trained as a product designer. This means that in theory I was able to design anything from a litter bin to a football stadium – both of which I did as a student. In the second year of my degree course something clicked. I became fascinated by how design creates the material world around us, and how design significantly contributes by default to how we make meaning of our world.

While I loved the notion that 'form follows function' (which inspires me to this day to live minimally), I became more interested in how 'form follows meaning', and how design is about transforming energy into form.

This was put to the test during the second year of my undergraduate degree course when we were asked to develop a series of new products for the Italian design factory, Alessi. Alberto Alessi himself came over to set up this student project, and we just fell in love with the beauty of their stainless steel kitchenware. His challenge to us was to imagine what next?

We worked in small groups, and it was the turn of my best friend and I to be team leaders. We struggled and struggled until eventually an insight just popped. What if we could harness the unfettered imagination of young children as our inspiration?

I phoned one of my parents' best friends, a head teacher, and a week later we were running a workshop in his primary school with five- and six-year-olds. In a few short minutes they produced the most amazingly unhindered visions of the future. We had our big idea and we entitled it 'Children's World'.

In the best way we knew how, our small student team generated ideas and three-dimensional models of kitchenware and related products to animate this new concept. We also wrote a research report. Alberto came over and we presented to him and it went well. We all noticed a glint in his eye when we shared our concept.

Not long after, Alessi launched a new range of 'child-like' products. They were beautiful and profound, and were executed way beyond our fledgling ability. With this new product range their business and brand seemed to explode with creativity, in turn becoming a household name.

I learned an important lesson (above and beyond the fact we should have negotiated some share options) that design had the power to transform businesses. Little did I know that designing business and organizational transformation was to become my life.

FIGURE 2.1 My Alessi sketch

FIGURE 2.2 Alessi "Family Follow Fiction"
Gino Zucchino sugar dispenser

02

WHAT IS NEEDED NOW?

Our world lacks clear leadership and it is changing faster than ever before. This is a cliché I know, and yet leaders would be wise to take heed. Technology is changing the game. Boundaries are blurring. Complexity is everywhere. Traditional jobs are eroding. Hyper-dependency continues to increase. Politics and big business have lost our trust, and to some their legitimacy. And, the media is trapped, lurching from one 'breaking news' event to the next, looking for who is to blame.

We are living and working through a period of quantum change.

So who's holding the container and space for us to move co-creatively into the future? It's not the G8 or the G20. It's not the UN. So who? It can't be the so-called superpowers. And, at the other end of the spectrum, it can't be smart mobs. Let's face it, we are already experiencing a crisis of leadership.

So what is needed now?

VUCA

'The future will continue to get more Volatile, Uncertain, Complex and Ambiguous'
Bob Johansen, Institute for the Future

From a creative perspective, profound shifts in context are opportunities to embrace rather than threats to minimize. We are living and working through a period of increased Volatility, Uncertainty, Complexity and Ambiguity – a VUCA world – and/or we are just becoming increasingly sensitive to these phenomena. Fortunately they are all critical ingredients for catalysing creative insight and collective breakthrough and therefore for evoking the music of innovation.

To disclose my stance early on, I *choose* to believe that we can innovate our way to more purposeful and vital futures. To do this we need to learn how to work with these phenomena and turn them into levers for profound change and transformation.

The danger of a VUCA world is that we can easily fall into fragmentation and protectionism. Yet, the inherent beauty of complexity and chaos is that it naturally re-patterns and re-orders. If we have the courage to hold the container for long enough, work through the discomfort of not knowing, and do not collapse spaces because of fear, impatience, insecurity or lack of skill then new patterns of thought and action emerge.

So what is needed now are leaders who can build social and organizational containers which are robust enough to hold us through periods of creative tension, as opposed to prematurely reacting to every presenting issue, and collapsing the tension at every turn.

GOVERNMENT

For example, in our hyper-connected world, politics will need to globalize as national governments struggle to keep up with the pace of change and face into the challenges of our time. To ensure a future role of import, cabinet governments will need to be:

- multi-stakeholder (beyond party politics, fragmented ministries and departments, and conflicting national interests);
- strategic (visionary and compelling as opposed to crisis-driven or problem-solving centric);
- purposeful yet agile;
- inclusive yet effective;
- digital and multi-channelled;
- and will need to continually earn and demonstrate their legitimacy in a fast-moving world.

To build trust, decisions will need to be followed up with elegant actions that are transparent, credible, reflective, courageous, vital and innovative; and that align with a clear and progressive moral framework that owns the costs and consequences of choice.

In the last five years alone, we have seen geopolitical, geo-economic and social change on a scale we have never experienced before. We have seen absolute revolution through the power of information. And we continue not to face up to the existential threat of climate change.

We need to find shared hope and common purpose.

We can no longer look to the United States to be the global saviour (if it ever was). It doesn't have the breadth of perspective or authority. No one country has. Instead we need international co-operation, on a new scale, and in new forms.

To this effect, policy-driven governance is too one-dimensional to solve the challenges we now face. We need trustworthy containers that enfold multi-stakeholders into spaces that catalyse new patterns of collective thought, behaviour and action.

Next, take the European Union, which has seen tough times recently with the euro crisis. Understandably there are many who are keen to stabilize the situation by seeking parity of contribution, and by increasing mechanisms of power and control.

What seems to be missing from the discussions is how to leverage the diversity of Europe. For a region that has a larger economy than the US or China, Europe hasn't yet got its head around how to leverage its diversity (of talent) as the engine room of innovation and as the key to Europe's energetic and ultimately economic recovery and sustainable growth. There is no other region in the world that has this bio-diverse hothouse at its disposal. And yet it is currently seen as Europe's greatest weakness, when in fact it is its greatest strength. When Europe learns to create a container potent enough to unify it in its diversity, then it will begin to realise its creative potential, and have a governing container it can be proud of.

What are needed now are containers that build trust, engage talent and embrace difference as the difference that makes the difference.

Creating containers and holding spaces on an international scale requires enormous amounts of energy. It requires visionary leaders, not political statesmen. And, we need to build these containers in business, education, civil society and unions. Then, and only then, will we be able to institutionalize the co-creative

FIGURE 2.3 Nested levels of resource

power of difference and discontinuity and build sustainable ecologies of both innovation and resource.

How leaders see and use resource is another indicator of their capability to build creative containers. I fondly remember one of the co-founders of **nowhere**, the late Michael Frye CBE, sharing his wisdom on the different mindsets around resource that he had encountered as an industrialist and a senior adviser to government. He saw four nested levels of 'resource' (Figure 2.3).

His model begins with leaders that see resource as *asset*. Their tendency is to *protect* their assets. This is a very current danger, as politicians and leaders tend to veer to being protectionist in their response to uncertainty.

Next, leaders see resource as *power*. The tendency of these leaders is to *control* power. For example, it is scarily common these days to see the truly remedial power plays that go on in (party) politics. It's like watching school kids arguing. It is embarrassing and, more importantly, it squanders opportunity for real progress!

A few leaders evolve to see resource as *talent*. Their challenge is to attract and *express* talent. To do this, leaders need to tell a bigger story, a story that values difference and paints inspiring pictures of a future in which we can all see our place and our contribution – a future where we will feel seen and appreciated.

And lastly, fewer leaders still learn to see resource as *energy*, and to purposefully *release* this energy into the world. To do this, they create containers and hold spaces that evoke the music of innovation, enabling us to operate at a higher and more co-creative level of consciousness.

BUSINESS

'Business has become, in this last half century, the most powerful institution on the planet. The dominant institution in any society needs to take responsibility for the whole'
– Willis Harman, World Business Academy

Whether we like it or not, business touches everyone on this planet. It is the main driver of societal change, and yet, business is fast reaching its own glass ceiling, where striving to do things 'better' is just not enough. Business needs to break through this ceiling to stay competitive, and to become a responsible pillar of society.

Take strategy, a business's ability to create and capture value through differentiated and sustainable competitive advantage. It is amazing how similar the strategic slide decks of global corporations are – the same diagnostics, the same four-box models, and the same future trends.

The irony is that strategy is all about leveraging difference and generating innovations. So why are organizations all using the same strategic methodologies, trapped and obsessed with extrapolating datasets from the past?

Similarly, the industrialized model of innovation is no longer working. What we think increases innovation actually suppresses it. For example, putting pressure on people to innovate just doesn't work unless we are also willing to transform our own view of risk, as illustrated in times of war. Most want innovation at no risk, unconsciously stifling creativity through cultures that can't handle or tolerate the inevitable iterations and failures associated with innovation.

It is important to remember that both strategy and innovation are actually messy and fuzzy activities. Denying this simply just dumbs them down.

I have also lost track of how often senior teams confuse strategy with strategic planning. The latter is useful in order to gain bottom-up data to help make tough decisions about the allocation of finite budgets and resources and to track implementation. But this is not strategy.

Better positioning, better processes and better people have become today's strategic table stakes. These are the basics. The real strategic challenge of our time is to out-innovate and to out-learn. More and more this means innovating and learning across and beyond organizational boundaries where different leadership rules apply.

Businesses are also confusing busyness with productivity. Leaders get stuck in endless meetings that add little or no value, painfully trying to get more and more from less. For some reason, they carry on doing what they've always done, pushing harder and harder, setting stretch goals and then stretching those.

This is just stupid.

What is needed now are new ways of thinking, relating, learning and organizing that enable organizations of all kinds to reconnect to their core purpose; and use this as an energetic and creative wellspring from which to generate and execute breakthrough strategies and innovations that shape futures fit for generations to come.

EDUCATION

As we look back up the human value chain we also see the need to break free of our western models of education, designed on the one hand to generate aristocrats, and on the other to produce blue-collar workers. Since the industrial revolution we have been incrementally building our educational systems on foundations from a bygone era, one that is scarily out of date. For example, there are very few jobs for life these days; and, what we are taught in our first year at university can be out of date by the time we graduate.

There are many great things about our educational systems, especially the abundance of dedicated teachers and leaders. But as educationalist Ken Robinson points out: 'As our children grow up we start to educate them progressively from the waist up. Then we focus on their heads, and slightly to one side.'

Our educational systems are designed to develop analytical, left-hemisphere intelligence, at the expense of developing (and even valuing) our emotional, physical, social and creative intelligences.

I would go further still, in that what is needed now are educational systems that teach us how to know ourselves (our talents, passions, dreams, hopes and fears), how to be curious, hungry learners; how to see beauty in diversity; how to develop multiple ways of knowing; how to appreciate our interconnectedness and interdependences; how to work with creative tension; how to explore new and novel intersections; and how to tap into the latent space between. These shouldn't be accidental outcomes of our educational systems; they should be core objectives.

While schools are actually very good at giving us a rounded knowledge base of the world, what is needed now are deeper journeys of self-discovery – enabling every child and young person to deep-dive into their sense of self, while learning how to build co-creative relationships with others, with their families and their communities, with the diversity of life, and with our planet.

Ultimately our challenge is to help our children learn how to see and embrace life as a creative adventure, where we are all (children, teachers, parents and leaders alike) prepared to be wrong, prepared to take risks, and prepared to wander with wonder.

HEALTH

'We live by the myth that stress is the enemy in our lives. The real enemy is our failure to balance stress with intermittent rest.'

– Tony Schwartz, The Energy Project

Some would say we are moving into the Well-Being era, while stress is on the increase, as of course is obesity. At every turn we are being invited to take a sugar rush or to load up on addictive carbohydrates. 'Craving' itself has become the drug of choice for many – craving for more, more, more – feeding our food, drugs, alcohol, shopping, money, status, celebrity and ego addictions. This is all wrong. Profoundly wrong. This cannot be the way that society realizes its highest potential and creative spirit.

Another addiction is busyness. As I've said earlier, busyness is often confused with productivity. Work harder. Work longer. Come on! Wake up! This is just unproductive and ludicrously unsustainable.

Let me give you an example of busyness. The most important characteristic I look for in organizational cultures is whether they are time rich or time poor. For me, there is a direct correlation between time rich organizations and those organizations that are innovating and shaping the future. Time rich doesn't mean slow or vacuous. Time rich is the ability to master time rather than be a victim of it. These leaders and organizations have learned how to speed up and slow down time. These cultures are often intense, vital, passionate, exciting and highly effective.

Juxtapose this against time poor organizations that predominantly have one pace – fast – where no one has any time. Some people find these types of environments addictive.

FIGURE 2.4 Time poor vs time rich

More and more are seeing through their unsustainability and ultimately their declining productivity.

One senior executive I know recently got out his PDA, clicked through to his diary and said: 'Look at this. Every hour I am in a different meeting.' And then he flicked through the days and weeks. 'And this happens every day. How can I add the value I am paid to add when I'm sitting in one-hour meetings all day, every day?'

This might be an extreme case. Literally this executive goes from one meeting to the next, in one-hour slots. Most of his peers and senior colleagues are also stuck in this pattern. We joke with them, as they are always six minutes late to meetings, roughly the time it takes to politely exit the previous meeting and get across the campus to the next meeting. As soon as they have settled down and energetically arrived, worked out what meeting they're in, and why they are there, it's time to move onto the next meeting. It's no surprise, therefore, that this organization is stuck having circular conversations. There's not enough time to get into the real issues, to get lost, to disagree, or to work with complexity, because of the pressure to get to tangible next actions before the meeting ends.

This is itself an interesting aside. When did the criteria for a successful meeting become a list of tangible next actions? As you'll see later, it's more often than not the intangibles that make the greatest difference.

Sometimes, no action at the end of a meeting is a good thing, if not a great thing! It doesn't mean you haven't been productive. Creating shared meaning takes time. Finding more elegant pathways requires incubation. The danger is that we become busy doing the wrong things, for busy-ness's sake; and that the successful use of our time is judged on tangible, and easily justifiable, criteria.

Another factor that contributes to this dynamic of busyness is the phenomenon of being overly inclusive – having the wrong people in the room, having everyman and their dog in the room, for fear of leaving someone or some function out. I've even seen executive teams want to undertake quite intense team development and insist that their personal assistants are in the room and even in some of the team activities. At one level this might sound progressive and innovative (and maybe I'm missing something) but in my view it's not. It's mad.

Now I am actually a fan of doing work with the personal assistants of the executive team, for they are a powerful group. However, to build a powerful team you need to establish the boundary of the team so as to increase its intimacy. Anything that diminishes this intimacy will by default dilute the co-creative potential of the team.

Being overly inclusive is a big trend at the moment. Often confused with, or justified by, being collaborative. This trend is a subtle way of diluting responsibility. It is also a way cultures evolve to avoid the emotional tension and the creative con-flicts inherent in making tough decisions and calling people to account. One organization I know reorganized themselves around their value chains. Each senior team now had all the key decision makers in the room, by design, in an attempt to speed up good decision making and to clarify accountabilities. No more than a few weeks after this re-org each of these 'value-chain' teams started setting up different committees so they didn't have to make the tough decisions themselves.

This type of organizational behaviour is often driven by a passive-fear, inherent within its culture; and can easily fall into being toxic, whereby people are polite to each other's face and quite cutting behind their backs. This is a way that some people attempt to claim power by trying to diminish other people's.

The massive cost of dysfunctional, unsafe and unhealthy cultures like these is how they subtly signal to their people that they should bring less and less of themselves to work. Work then becomes workmanlike as the workplace becomes a battleground of intellectual and political power plays. The critical place and creative power of emotion, and in turn creative tension, becomes suppressed, as they are perceived as being too exposing for senior leaders.

These types of leaders and cultures are then surprised when morale is low, stress is high and innovation is stifled. Some don't care.

From my experience, high morale and high innovation invite and excite us to bring more of ourselves to work, not less.

It is no surprise, therefore, that the root of the word 'health', is also the root of the word 'wholeness'. What is needed now are leaders who can help us bring our wholeness – our intellectual, emotional, social, physical, and purposeful selves – to work on a daily basis.

TECHNOLOGY

'Technology is now part and parcel of every problem and every solution.'

– Jared Cohen, Director of Google Ideas

Leaders need to accept that technology is omnipresent. Technology has undergone a metamorphosis. It is no longer just an enabler. Change, innovation, transformation and revolution happen in real-time, are non-linear and embedded. Our interconnected world enables us to amplify, accelerate and cross-pollinate at the push of a button.

For example, a couple of years ago I would have said that communication technology (video-conferencing and webinars) could never substitute true, face-to-face meetings; for it's the quality of face-to-face contact that makes all the difference. Despite progress with this technology (for example, Tele Presence is amazing), I would still argue that it's the quality of conversation that's the key – whether real or virtually assisted. You can still have a poor conversation or meeting over great video-conferencing technology (as you can *face to face*). At present these new technologies don't make you more skilful, more self-aware, or help you hold the creative tension in the space between you needed to catalyse creative insight and collective breakthrough. While we are making huge strides in technology, we are still slow in embracing the revolution that is happening in human process design.

What excites me are the possibilities that arise when we combine technology with human process design. Having seen some of the communication technology that is in the pipe-line, I believe that technology will soon be able to facilitate better conversations and creative exchanges than the three-dimensional world that we normally occupy. What is coming is truly amazing. The way we think about and design different types of meetings (weaving together both human process and dynamic content) will transform beyond recognition. We have only scratched the surface of what technology will bring, how it will pervade our work and life, and what this means for leadership and innovation.

CREATIVE TALENT AND GENERATION Y

'Meritocracy, camaraderie, non-traditional, integration of work and personal life, fierce independence ... these are the values of Generation Y.'

– Knoll

A further example, among many other possible examples, of the shifting context of leadership is how creative talent and Generation Y are becoming ever more vital ingredients in helping leaders and their organizations traverse the emerging future. Creative talent and Gen Y naturally move towards meaning and purpose and have the innate ability to wander in the unknown, to get lost and have the presence of mind to stand still and allow the new to emerge. Furthermore, they also have a creative fire within them, ideal to fuel change, innovation and transformation.

Add into the mix the digital, native traits of the millennial generation, where smart mobs and creative commons are just the way things are. They're tremendously bright, super-fast, naturally entrepreneurial and profoundly naïve – naïve in the sense of unencumbered. The danger is that past experience is not passed on because Gen X doesn't know how to share its knowledge with Gen Y without patronising them, and because Gen Y has very little trust or belief in Gen X.

What is needed now is to help Generation Y become un-imaginably wise.

SUPER-WICKED PROBLEMS

We also cannot deny the super-wicked problems of our time: climate change; poverty; water, food & energy scarcity; the economic system... The inherent challenges of super-wicked problems are that the people trying to solve them created them in the first place, that time is not on our side, and that we are in danger of making decisions that our future selves wouldn't want us to make.

Super-wicked problems are deeply systemic, based on ingrained habits, behaviours and beliefs and/or the long-term cost and unintended consequences thereof.

We will continue to struggle to break through these problems unless we learn to build containers large enough, and strong enough, to allow new patterns of thought and action to emerge, while evoking us to let go of old ways of behaving.

At the end of the day, all the elements of the emerging context I have outlined, and others that there just isn't space to cover, are creative challenges that we need to square up to. What is needed is a different level of political, commercial, educational and technological consciousness. Unfortunately this level of consciousness is rare, if unheard of, in politicians. Transformational containers are built upon trust and the perception of trust, and most politicians seem untrustworthy. To address these super-wicked problems we will need to face into how structurally (and sometimes morally) corrupt our political systems are, and where their short-term agendas continue to undermine the revolutions that are needed in business, education, health and governance itself.

THE GROWTH DILEMMA

These super-wicked problems require us to challenge some of our biggest assumptions. One of the biggest assumptions that intrigues me is what I call the 'growth dilemma'.

Our societies are built upon the premise of growth, and that growth is king. Businesses are only seen as successful if they are in a growth phase – likewise economies. The need to grow, to generate greater revenues, more profit, more GDP, is a blind addiction.

So how does this insatiable hunger for growth align with the fact that our planet is by default a finite resource? More, more, more is not only unsustainable, it's simply not possible. At some point growth stops working, and the paradigm breaks down.

There are two main (archetypal) responses to this inevitable breakdown. The first is, 'Oh my God, the world is going to be a horrible, dark, scary place – socially, environmentally, culturally and financially. The rich will get richer and the poor poorer. Social divides, unrest and ultimately conflicts will increase. A minority will flourish, at the expense of the majority. Different value sets and beliefs will separate and fragment society as tolerance levels decrease based on underlying fears.' These may come true, and maybe we've already caught glimpses of this potential future.

The second archetypal response is to choose to look into our deepest assumptions and fears, to hold them up for challenge and enquiry, while seeking other more sustainable and purposeful social constructs.

To build containers strong enough to hold the intensity of this challenge, we must first paint pictures of possible futures that we want to shape, build and move towards together.

The danger with this second response is that we can fall into the realm of idealism and/or become obsessed with what's wrong and with what's not working.

However, if we believe this second option is actually an option, then innovation is the key to this future. To bastardize a classic line from Star Wars – 'Obi-Wan Kenobi, you're our only hope' – innovation is our only hope, and was ever thus.

INNOVATION AS THE KEY

A recent article in HBR by Scott D Anthony (2012) describes how we are now catching glimpses of what he calls 'fourth-era innovation'. In his model: first-era innovation is centred around the lone inventor; second-era innovation is based upon the impact of corporate labs and hothouses, like Bell or HP Labs; and third-era innovation refers to the era of venture capitalism and its focus on business process and business model innovation. He then describes fourth-era innovation as the emergence of 'transformational catalysts' who challenge organizational assumptions, work against the grain, and through persistence shape and pioneer new business models.

I too believe there is a fourth-era of innovation – I call it the *fourth realm*. For us this realm is about building cultures of innovation, of which transformational catalysts are one part of the puzzle. Moreover, these cultures can transcend organizational boundaries and become strange attractors to wider ecosystems of current and future stakeholders.

Fourth-realm innovation is only possible when there is a purposeful container which values difference, self-awareness, quality of contact and relationship, new and novel intersections, creative tension, the power of creative teams and communities, and evocative leadership. Moreover, these containers are designed to shift the frequency at which we think, learn, relate and organize – simultaneously leveraging individual uniqueness and collective intelligence.

Now, to jump back briefly to the growth dilemma, I realize I am portraying an overly simplistic view on many fronts. I realize that economics are a measure of progress and contribution, and that competition in many ways aids innovation.

I am a believer in change, and that standing still is not an option. Moreover, I am a believer in human growth and human potential, in that we are born into existence to learn how to be all that we can be, and that progress is part of the human spirit.

So what's the paradigm beyond growth for growth's sake?

This is an important question and conundrum for us to hold. It challenges us to review our beliefs, our social constructs, and our mental models.

For us to innovate around this question we first need to invest in expanding our creativity. And, to expand our creativity requires us to evolve our consciousness. As I've outlined, this is not just an individual endeavour, it is a collective one too. How do we, our families, our organizations, our governments, our communities learn to become more creative in our being? And who will step forward and lead us there?

This is not about the hero leader. Rather it is about the containers and spaces that leaders can learn to create and hold for us, so we can genuinely surprise ourselves with what we can achieve.

There has to be a different paradigm, and it must start with a shift in our individual and collective consciousness. I don't mean that in any happy-clappy new age way. I mean a fundamental re-patterning of what we believe to be 'success', and will undoubtedly include a shift in self-image, and more interestingly a shift in communal-image.

QUALITY OF CONSCIOUSNESS

'In the past we have seen two types of business strategies: those based on differentiation and those based on cost. In the future we will see two types of organizations. The first one is a group of lean and mean efficiency machines without a soul, organizations that don't connect to the deeper aspirations of *their investors, employees, partners, customers, communities, and managers. The second one is a group of organizations that are more inspired, mindful, and purpose-driven. That purpose can be articulated in many ways, but its bottom line concerns the well-being of all.'*

– Otto Scharmer (2011)

As I've mentioned before, talent moves towards purpose and meaning and less so towards money for money's sake. Knowing how to build purpose-driven organizations is becoming increasingly important for businesses that want and need to innovate to survive and thrive. Like a strange attractor, purpose attracts talent.

In the last few years I have been contacted by numerous CEOs about the accelerating changes and wider shifts in context that their businesses are having to traverse. Some are starting to see and feel their way into it, as I will outline later, with more post-conventional strategies and visions. And in the same breath they admit that the tools that they have accumulated in their metaphoric backpacks are insufficient for pulling these more complex futures into the present. Intellect and experience are no longer enough.

Being ahead of the curve, these progressive CEOs know they need to invest in new leadership capabilities and skills. Fortunately, this group also see leadership as a lifelong endeavour.

Most of the leaders that I am referring to are in their 50s and 60s, experienced, wise and surprisingly humble.

Another type of leader is also fast emerging – the young executive leader, often in their 40s. I call them young CEOs. They're smart, sharp, quick, bright and full of energy. They have their blogs and they work all hours. These young CEOs often fall into a number of traps, including making their predecessors wrong, micro-managing their direct reports, isolating themselves socially, rejecting professional support mechanisms (as these are all seen as signs of weakness) and claiming power through fear. They are unwilling to admit they don't know, and so 'their way' becomes 'the way'. This is compounded by the fact they don't believe in having challenging sounding boards around them to help them orientate and contextualize their thoughts. This is dangerous leadership.

While bright and amenable on the outside to occasional colleagues, with those they work with regularly their tendency is to dominate – intellectually, behaviourally and of course positionally. This often leads to the executive team being run as a hub and spoke, single leader work group.

In turn, the next few levels down in the organization begin to see the power of the executive team, as a team, diminish. Everyone takes their cues from the CEO, or from a leader of one of the feuding political camps that naturally emerge underneath this type of leadership style.

> 'The blind spot of current leadership and systems theory is consciousness. It is the quality of consciousness and awareness that drives the quality of results.'
>
> – Otto Scharmer (2011)

Now, it's not intellect that makes a great leader – although it helps. Rather it's the quality of their consciousness – their personal and systemic awareness. This arises from knowing that how we see the world can only ever be based on our own filters, lenses and biases. There is no one truth. We can only look at things from where we are.

Walking through the world creatively requires multiple perspectives because it's in the weave that innovation happens. This quality of consciousness recognizes that we do not understand what we see; rather we see what we understand. The world can only, therefore, be subjective. Mastery requires us to enquire consciously into this subjectivity, to realize that we have been conditioned to look through our consciousness and not at it.

This level of self-awareness, or presence, refers to an ability to be still. Unfortunately lots of bright leaders are unable to be still. They fall into the habit of completing other people's sentences, or second-guessing where conversations are going, anything that takes them out of the present. Their impatience challenges people to get to the point. This means they miss the fragile emergence of newness – how to see it, coax it, nurture it and grow it.

And, just to be fair, some of these young CEOs are in a class of their own. Their brilliance is more than intellectual. Their challenge, however, is to close the capability gap between themselves and their direct reports – as opposed to revelling in the gap.

SUMMARY

The World Economic Forum Global Agenda Council on New Models of Leadership calls the emerging future 'a quantum shift in context'. This shift is affecting both governments and businesses alike. The rules of the game are changing and we are just beginning to feel into what this all means.

What is needed now is for us to develop:

- Social and organizational containers that are robust enough to hold us through periods of creative tension, as opposed to reacting to every presenting issue, and collapsing tension at every turn.

- Governing systems that tap into the collective intelligence of the whole.

- Organizing systems that embrace difference as the difference that makes the difference.

- New ways of thinking, relating, learning and organizing that enable organizations of all kinds to reconnect to their core purpose, and then use it as an energetic and creative wellspring from which to generate breakthrough strategies and innovations.

- Leaders who can help us bring our wholeness – our intellectual, emotional, social, physical, and purposeful selves – to work on a daily basis.

- Educational systems that support a deeper journey of self-discovery – enabling every child and young person to deep-dive into their sense of self, and learn how to build co-creative relationships with others, with their families and communities, with the diversity of life, and with our planet.

- A creative synthesis between digital technology and human process design.

- Ways to help Generation Y become unimaginably wise.

- A shift in our individual and collective consciousness.

So how can leaders of all kinds embrace these developmental needs?

These changes are both dramatic and exciting. Without the emergence of new leadership models (and more importantly new leadership practices) that understand that objective, mechanical and Newtonian worldviews are no longer full representations of the world in which we live, we will remain stuck, banging our heads against the glass ceiling. This ceiling is 'us' getting in our own way, blindly arguing from and for our own limitations.

New leadership models and practices are needed now to help us step over a critical threshold – personally, organizationally and societally. This threshold has been referred to by some as a threshold of ego-development – a movement in our awareness, from a conventional, objective and fragmented view of the world, to a more post-conventional, subjective and interdependent view of the world.

It is only through a shift in our consciousness that new external possibilities, resources, innovations and pathways become knowable and available to us. New models of leadership need to illuminate this critical threshold, while also challenging leaders to muster the humility, energy and wisdom to step forward and over it.

STEPPING IN

I'm a B-Boy at heart. I grew up in the Eighties with break-dancing and hip-hop. I found breaking (breakdancing) an amazing outlet to express my creativity. It required weeks and weeks of practice to either master or invent a move. It was about total dedication.

I remember very clearly being asked for the first time to join a crew to 'battle' against another crew. There were loads of people standing in a circle. In the middle of this crowd, facing off, were the two crews. Both were much older and bigger than me, and to be honest I was out of my depth. Then, all of a sudden, one of the opposing crew members started body-popping his way across the circle, gliding and locking.

Now remember, I had never been in this situation before, so I imagine in one sense I was caught observing it for the first time. This guy (kid to be precise) came close enough to pretend to take my head from my shoulders and bounce it around like a basketball. This was his way of challenging me.

Now in that moment of sheer and total panic – I remember it well – I had a choice. Either I step in or I step out. If I stepped in the risk was humiliation and failure. If I stepped out the risk was humiliation and failure. So I had nothing to lose. I stepped in. I cannot for the life of me remember anything from that moment on, other than I stepped in. I imagine I tried my best, and I was probably okay. But I had stepped in!

To this day I use my memory of this choice-point to resource me when I'm at my edge as a practitioner. I am paid to help people find and step over their edge, for this is what creativity, innovation, change and transformation are all about in practice (not theory). How can I expect others to step over this edge if I can't or won't?

I choose to believe that if they jump into the unknown I'll jump with them. That for me is the nature of true co-creation.

Yet we all have a choice. We should always weigh up the risks and the rewards. If the only risk is failure (and nobody gets hurt or shamed) there should be no choice.

FIGURE 3.1 Yes, that's me on the floor. My best angle

03

A MOVEMENT OVER A SUBTLE THRESHOLD

Over the last 15 years I have specialized in building cultures of innovation with and for our partners and clients. These transformational journeys often take multiple years, as we traverse the subtle phases and stages of building these types of cultures. It requires leaders to have foresight (because culture change has a time lag), courage (because it means taking yourself and many others out of their comfort zone), and conviction (because you need to stay the course when you disturb the status quo, and resist collapsing back to what you already know).

I feel very privileged to have been given the opportunity and support to help design and catalyse these exciting and compelling journeys. I have learned a lot about the sequence of building blocks, the choreography of interventions and the non-negotiables, what could be simplified and omitted, and what conditions maximize sustainable success.

I've also learned that there is an art to building cultures of innovation. The subtlety of this art lies in meeting senior leaders where they are, dealing with a variety of scales and complexities, embracing diverse cultures, languages and legacies, and of course adapting to different industries and sectors.

But there are also a number of generic principles to building cultures of innovation. One of which is the time it takes to shift a cultural pattern – almost irrelevant to the size of the company. In my experience, this means companies from 4,000 to 80,000 employees. I'm sure timescales can be reduced with small- and medium-sized companies, but this is not where my experience lies.

Another principle is to seek out at least one, ideally two, post-conventional leaders in the client team, hopefully including the CEO. Within this context, 'post-conventional' refers to a level of awareness as outlined by Ken Wilber's (1995) model of Consciousness, which in turn inspired ego-development models by Jane Loevinger (1998) and Susanne R Cook-Greuter (2005), and the Action Logics levels of William Torbert and David Rooke (2000). Torbert and Rooke go further in their research to propose that organizational transformation requires two or more senior leaders to have evolved into and be able to operate from this post-conventional realm.

From many studies, Torbert and Rooke propose that only about 15 per cent of their sample populations have moved into the post-conventional realm. This is particularly true in the West, where society mostly sees the highest stage of conventional ego-development – the Achiever – as the pinnacle of development and thereby success.

Having worked with these frameworks for many years, my own experience would align with the premise that those leaders that have been most successful at leading organizational transformations (including cultural shifts) are able to tap into and operate from the post-conventional realm.

Moreover, I would propose that this movement from a conventional to post-conventional worldview is the threshold that

WILBER Consciousness Model	COOK-GREUTER Ego-Development Stages	TORBERT & ROOKE Action Logic Levels
SOUL Transcendent / Unitive View	Unitive	9. Ironist
	Construct Aware	8. Magician
VISION LOGIC Systemic View	Autonomous	7. Strategist
	Individualist	6. Individualist
Post-Conventional Threshold		
MIND Conventional	Conscientious	5. Achiever
	Self-Conscious	4. Expert
	Conformist	3. Diplomat
BODY Pre-Conventional	Self-Defensive	2. Opportunist
	Impulsive	1. Impulsive

FIGURE 3.2 Models of post-conventional consciousness

organizational cultures, teams and leaders need to step over in order to create containers and hold spaces potent enough and large enough to:

- catalyse creative insight and collective breakthrough;
- face into the super-wicked problems of society;
- and ultimately, evoke the music of innovation – thereby enabling us all to live and work at a higher, co-creative frequency.

Informed and inspired by the models outlined above, and from similar developmental models by Gregory Bateson (1972), Roger Benson (1991), Harrison Owen (1990) and others... **nowhere** developed a simple, four-stage framework of nested layers, designed to help organizational cultures, teams and leaders step over this threshold and learn to operate from a post-conventional worldview. I referred to it earlier as a move into the fourth realm – referring to the fourth nested layer.

Each layer of the framework describes a significantly ex-panded worldview, while still containing the previous ones as nested sub-sets. Each new layer has its own coherent modes of thinking, relating, learning and organizing. And each new layer has its own strengths and weaknesses.

As we evolve through these four nested layers, some of the key indicators we look for include:

- how we are making meaning of the world around us;
- our level of self-awareness;
- our sense of belonging and quality of relationship with others;
- our capacity to work with difference and integrate differences;

- our ability to work with the unknown – unconscious, invisible, intangible and implicate;
- our sense of humour; and
- our capacity to work with different forms and degrees of complexity.

The threshold that I am most interested in is the shift from the third layer to the fourth realm – the move from conventional to post-conventional. It is not a movement in skill, rather one of expanded *voltage* and what we will later outline as an increase in *capacity*. Together, voltage and capacity enable us to affect frequency.

THE EVOLUTION OF ORGANIZATIONAL CULTURES

Organizational cultures are founded by default on being *opportunist*. They are born of seeing a gap in the market, a window of opportunity, a new need or possibility.

Opportunist cultures have a full-on energy, where emotions run very high or very low. Naivety is both an asset and a hindrance in this first layer, as misunderstanding the norms and rules of the game, or intentionally breaking them, generates new business possibilities.

Loyalty is to their latest idea.

Some of the limitations of these cultures include a fragility, a liability for emotional over-reaction and a tendency to value the individual over the collective.

If these cultures survive they then seek out more knowledge and more know-how. Their focus shifts to the process of turning their ideas into products, in order to keep ahead of the competition. This is the realm of the *expert* culture.

Expert cultures are capable of engaging with greater complexity and abstraction. They are fact and data driven, and often hold a scientific lens to the world, so that only 'truths' bubble to the surface. These cultures have an objective view of the world as something out there and separate from them. It needs to be tangible and measurable. Their loyalty is ultimately to their vocation, to their science.

Another limitation of these cultures is that they don't know when good is enough. They strive for perfection at the cost of action. They can also be extremely conservative, waiting for more and more data so as to discover the right answer. To this effect these cultures often create avoiding mechanisms and structures to pass on or dilute accountability and to abdicate decision making. This includes finding it difficult, if not impossible, to stop projects and initiatives.

In danger of skipping ahead too quickly, I remember visiting a post-conventional culture and being told a story about how they held a party in the company canteen for their whole organization, just because a team had had the courage to stop a project. The belief and total conviction of the team had been to stop and reallocate resource so as to better serve the business's core purpose.

Finally, expert cultures are highly rational, often with a social awkwardness. A number of distinctive sub-cultures can form around different scientific and/or functional expertises, resulting in the conscious and unconscious subversion of the 'other' – and, an unwillingness to listen to or work with those outside of your 'tribe'.

The next cultural layer is a movement to commercialize knowledge and know-how. These are *achiever* cultures. They are action-orientated, obsessed with high performance, benchmarking and measurement and their primary motivation is money.

FIGURE 3.3 Cultural layers

These cultures break organizations into bits while recognizing the need for the parts to work in unison, like a machine, in order to create and capture the greatest value. Diversity is tolerated and leveraged in service of a common ideology and/ or a shared endeavour.

Problem solving is the name of the game, while the Holy Grail is creating more from less. The glass is always half full in achiever cultures, as opposed to half empty in expert cultures. Social context is intentionally expanded in order to deliver the best results and to focus on scaling and replicating. There is always a sense of push in achiever cultures as their loyalty is to 'success'.

These cultures can easily fall into being very aggressive and macho, where you are only as good as your last sale, campaign or quarterly result.

While expert cultures can become very comfortable, achiever cultures can be driven by a passive or active fear, making them culturally unsafe to challenge the status quo. This in turn leads people in achiever cultures to do one of two things. Either to lose their sense of self, to work all hours, and in doing so reduce their sense of identity to their job, their role and their work; or, to separate their work from their life, such that their job is no more than a means to an end, for earning money, while they wait for the weekend.

Most cultures get stuck at this stage, as over time achiever cultures erode organizational creativity. Creative tension is collapsed at every opportunity in case it reveals the vulnerabilities of key leaders. Innovation is turned into the management of a process, with tunnels, funnels and stage-gates. And, performance management becomes an obsession. Leaders then wonder why their innovation pipelines are running drier than desired.

In a bid to increase performance costs are cut, finance functions start to gain too much power, and re-engineering and restructuring become the default intervention. It is sad for me to say, but I have lost count of the number of global corporations that have reached a ceiling of imagination and creativity and then slide into countless years of restructuring. The even sadder part of the story is the impact this has on the people who get stuck in these cycles of restructuring, constantly flipping between feeling their way into a new restructure and waiting for the next. It's simply remedial.

While an important card to play once in a while, restructuring is massively over-used, and scarily all too often recommended by large management consultancies. This is a sign that the executive leaders have lost the plot and have only a one-dimensional view of change and transformation. This vicious cycle rips the heart and soul out of a company's culture. And it is horrible to witness.

Now, before I move on to the fourth realm, let me emphasize again that each of these nested layers are needed. Organizations need opportunists, experts and achievers. Indeed the latter two are the engine room of good business. They are just not enough to truly shape the future, to out-innovate the competition, and to become a great business.

The fourth realm is therefore what we call the *innovator/shaper* layer. It is a movement from the conventional into the post-conventional. It is the most significant and most subtle worldview shift for cultures to make.

At this threshold there is a realization that the meaning of things depends upon one's relative position and therefore interpretation. These cultures start to raise their awareness to the phenomenon that they only see what they understand, and that they are limited by their conditioned frames of reference.

Language and meaning become more fluid as they fold the intangible and the subjective into their collective worldview. They come to know that their worldview is only ever constructed.

Meaning-making and language become more playful as they learn that innovation isn't a linear process, or a fact-based decision-making activity; rather it is about making marks in the world and allowing new patterns and possibilities to emerge in the space between. They therefore consciously call upon other ways of knowing, beyond the rational, to include feelings, intuitions and embodied knowing. They know that without these extended capacities it is very difficult to hold complexity, integrate difference, challenge fundamental assumptions and creatively scrutinize deeply held beliefs.

Analysing the world by breaking it up into parts is useful in previous layers but inelegant in the fourth realm. This realm choreographs wholes. Unlike the achiever culture that focuses on alignment, the innovator/shape culture is about attunement. They work together like an orchestra, creating music with their different instruments, gifts and talents, such that their resonance is greater than the sum of the parts. This is why there is a creative hum to cultures of innovation. It's palpable.

These cultures also orientate themselves around burning questions. They relish creative tension. They understand that innovation happens at new and novel intersections. They are deeply purposeful. And they invest in and destroy structures only in service of the creative process.

From the fourth realm the organization is seen as a 'container' in which to release our creative energy and potential. This container is designed to enable the other nested layers/worldviews to work as a co-creative ecology. For example, experts and achievers often don't gel. Experts can easily become victims of the more commercial, action-orientated achievers. Achievers see themselves as earning the money while the experts spend it. The default position is for achievers to dominate and for the experts to feel resentful. The truth is that their worldviews are simply different, making it difficult for them to meet dynamically in the middle. This two-tiered dynamic makes innovation workmanlike at best.

Innovator/shaper cultures consciously and unconsciously create environments in which these different sub-cultures can embrace, leverage and appreciate their differences as part of an integrated, co-creative whole.

Moreover, with practice, this container can be expanded beyond organizational boundaries to combine innovative ecologies of external stakeholders and partners – present and future – moving them beyond transactional, linear and dependent relationships.

An important challenge and danger with explaining this threshold is that we come up against the limitations of language. Achievers often struggle with the subtle and the intangible. This is akin to the limitations of some strategic planning processes. When a truly great strategy has been created, its downfall is often because the strategy is then interpreted through the orthodoxies of the dominant culture such that any creative genius in the strategy is simply and literally 'lost in translation'.

Before I dive a little deeper into the nature and qualities of cultures of innovation (operating from the fourth realm) I would like to share how these nested layers also play out in teams and through leadership.

THE EVOLUTION OF TEAMS

How teams meet is a measure of the dominant, cultural worldview, as well as the level of consciousness of the leader. Let me take you through the nested layers from a team perspective.

The first layer is called the *pseudo* team. This is the most rudimentary form of team. Arguably it's not a team, rather a group of (dis-)associated individuals. The only thing they have in common is that they report to the same person. The leader will have one-to-one relationships with everyone and most decisions will be taken during bilateral encounters with the leader. Relationships between 'team' members are professionally shallow. If discussion topics are relevant to more than one member of the team a sense of protectionism can easily kick in around one's fiefdom. This leads to a competitive dynamic between team members even though their areas of responsibility are completely different.

These teams are disconnected (as a team, not necessarily as individual leaders) from the people they lead. When people come to present to the team, they often walk away de-energized, having witnessed its dysfunction at play.

Unfortunately, these teams are less rare than you would imagine, and I'm sure some of these traits sound familiar.

The next and most common form of team is the *operational* team. These teams are characterized by having long agendas. Most operational teams sit around a large table, where members habitually sit in their usual chairs.

In extreme cases, operational (expert) teams hold their meetings around a U-shaped table. The leader will sit at the bottom of the U, with the rest of the team fanning out from the leader on both sides of the U based on their level of seniority. People are then traipsed in to present at a screen at the top of the U.

Operational meetings are mostly driven by PowerPoint presentations, ie the majority of the time is spent listening to inputs, making these meetings ultra-rational in nature. Information is king in this world. Experts see information as power and their tendency is to control it. Moreover, these meetings

FIGURE 3.4 Team layers

can become rather indulgent in nature, as experts are addicted to wanting more and more information.

These meetings can be good for managing the delivery of the day-to-day, and for overseeing governance issues. In essence, the norm is updates, followed by Q&A, feedback and/or a decision. There is usually limited time in operational meetings for exchange of views or creative exploration as the team is focused on working down a long list of agenda items.

The downside of this meeting format is that the leader is the only one who can hold the wider pattern, as they are the only one that has the back-story to each input. There is therefore little or no awareness, let alone use of, a wider collective intelligence. This, together with having the positional advantage of being at the centre of the team, means the leader controls the meeting, and everyone and everything pivots around them.

The next team is the *strategic* team. This is a team whereby the leader has stepped out of the metaphorical centre of the team to create a space for them to collectively work the tricky issues, business dilemmas and areas of strategic conflict. Inputs in these meetings are about sharing data and analysis. This creates the context for critical discussions and important trade-offs.

These meetings are about optimizing performance and results. They are about identifying priorities and managing risk. Cause and effect is debated in order to get to reasoned, informed and fact-based decisions.

Goals and targets are set, as numbers and time motivate. These teams are enormously conscientious, often working all hours. Allegiance is split between the leader (through positional power and loyalty) and to the best result for the company. This can lead, if there is a safe enough container, to great debates around different strategic scenarios.

Strategic agendas and roadmaps are the currency of these teams, turning strategic intent into strategic pillars, pillars into

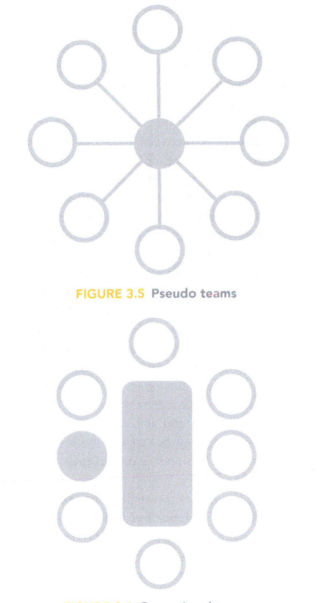

FIGURE 3.5 Pseudo teams

FIGURE 3.6 Operational teams

objectives, objectives into growth levers, growth levers into KPIs, KPIs into initiative and projects, and projects into metrics. These teams measure everything. Having data about everything is what this worldview is all about. It's the data that tells us what the right thing to do is. The downside of this is it leads to strategy by numbers.

An extreme example of this came in the form of excessive reliance on value-based management. A big fad in the 1990s, using VBM as the dominant tool in decision making can be an awesome way of taking the life and soul out of a company's culture. Managing solely by numbers may appear to create and extract value for shareholders over the short term but is highly unlikely to create the conditions for growth through innovation for the mid and long term.

Fortunately, most strategic teams are bright enough to have moved beyond a solely numbers-based approach, to also look at how they manage some of the other key multipliers of value – learning, innovation, and talent … as well as great strategy itself.

Some strategic teams can also edge towards the post-conventional realm, especially when they start to realize that their job is not just about coming up with the answers but also the critical questions – questions that animate, excite, stretch and galvanize energy in and across their organization. This means admitting that they don't know the answer to some things, and that 'not-knowing' is part of great strategy and great leadership.

Again, as we move from conventional to post-conventional it is important to remember that the challenge here is not to be trapped in one mode of team. Each layer is nothing more than an archetype, and these layers are not mutually exclusive. While teams generally have a dominant *modus operandi*, some might drift between two or more of these conventional forms. Most, however, are blind to the possibility and potential of the fourth realm. This is the realm of the *creative* team.

FIGURE 3.7 Strategic teams

Creative teams are the DNA of cultures of innovation. While the previous layers focus on leveraging, ordering and controlling the known (facts, figures and data), creative teams are able to embrace and work with the unknown, the intangible, the invisible, the unconscious and the implicate.

Meetings no longer require delivery skills and now require discovery skills. This is why stepping over the threshold to becoming a creative team is so difficult for achievers. Their success to date is likely to be based on their ability to deliver results in the known. Their challenge now is to wander with wonder into the unknown.

The entry-level skills for being a creative team have been documented by many. They include questioning, observing, networking and experimenting. For example, the ability to:

- Question the status quo and to challenge key assumptions and beliefs.

- Observe with a beginner's mind.

- Network into the new and novel intersections (the knots, nets and threads) of diverse experiences and knowledge.

- And, to fail faster through experimentation to succeed sooner.

While each of the previous layers develop innovations in their own way, they are but echoes of the insights and breakthroughs that are possible from a creative team.

Creative teams are formed around a quest – or quest-ion. This quest-ion points them into the unknown while generating a creative fire, a passion and a tension in the team. These teams relish the challenge of breaking free of current reality and breaking through into a new reality, such that their view of the world reorders. This allows what was previously hidden and unavailable to be seen for the first time.

So what does it take to break free and to break through, for it is easy to say, and difficult to do? This is where innovation becomes a true corporate art form, as opposed to being reduced to the management of a process, as is the orthodoxy of the achiever.

Managing the flow of innovation is important if there is already an abundance of innovative possibilities (beyond lots of ideas). However, no matter how well you manage this process, it won't generate innovation per se, even when we layer in current tools like 'idea jamming'. Jamming is great at generating loads of ideas through the dominant cultural lens. In this instance, incremental change happens through a sheer numbers game, and breakthrough happens, if at all, by complete accident, not by design.

Creative teams on the other hand enjoy diving into messy and fuzzy space. To do this they tune into themselves – both individually and collectively. Team members then intentionally expand their self-awareness to embrace and tune into other ways of knowing, beyond the intellect; and, then see and work overtly with the diverse talents (beyond role) of each team member.

Creative teams deepen the quality of their relationships in order to leverage their diversity and hold creative tension. To this effect, the potency of a creative team is to the power of **n** – where **n** is the number of people in the team. This is in contrast to the strategic team that has more of an accumulative effect rather than a multiplier effect.

A colleague of mine, Chris Jacob, describes how creative teams can step into a peak experience that he calls 'our beautiful mind'. This is when he believes a team is able to activate and access over 90 per cent of the total number of available combinations of creative relationships and intersections across its members. At this point they move into a creative hive-like mind (not to be confused with group-think), where a larger collective intelligence becomes accessible. This is where the creative team is able to see new pattern in complexity, new order in chaos, and where innovative foregrounds start to emerge from strategic backgrounds.

In general, creative teams are not permanent structures. Senior leadership teams can learn to step into a creative team form for limited periods of time, before appropriately dropping back into strategic and operational team forms to map, prioritize and execute. More often, creative teams live and die around specific questions and endeavours, where their job is to break free and break through on behalf of the wider organization or ecosystem. They come into being and burn brightly for a while, so as to shine light on the new, the previously unimagined and the unseen. Moreover, members of creative teams who have experienced collective breakthrough are then able to use their expanded worldview as an evocative resource to enfold others in the optimal way forward, minimizing the 'lost in translation' effect and the usual organizational resistance to change.

THE EVOLUTION OF LEADERSHIP

Bill Isaacs, the founder and president of the Boston-based consulting firm Dialogos and senior lecturer at MIT's Sloan Business School, shared an important principle with me many years ago. He said, 'You can only transform an organizational system proportionate to the size of the core leadership container being held at the top.'

As an external, I've learned how to help executive and senior teams create and hold core leadership containers that are large enough for an ecology of internal teams to step over into the fourth realm. I've seen executive teams learn how to

FIGURE 3.8 Creative teams

step over this threshold at will and with skill. I've also seen some executive leaders live over this threshold in a place of unconscious competence. Somehow they have acquired the subtle skills needed to operate in the fourth realm without knowing it. Fewer still have codified their capacity to operate in the fourth realm as conscious competence, enabling them to pass on their wisdom.

For some reason, I am particularly fascinated by leaders that unconsciously work from the fourth realm, as it seems so antithetical. What follows this group of special leaders is a fear from their organizations that the magic they clearly and tangibly create around them will be lost once they leave or retire. These leaders and organizations get stuck in a conundrum whereby they fear codifying this magic in case it somehow collapses the quantum, and yet know that if they don't the magic will disappear anyway.

There is another real danger here. I have seen many businesses try to migrate the magical cultural ingredients of a newly acquired organization into the mothership.

Unfortunately, what happens more often than not is the replication of the conscious competences that people espouse to be the magic ingredients, totally missing the unconscious competences that are the actual magic ingredients. This leads to a truly painful period of remedial change management and behavioural dictates from the top. It is so frustrating to watch as they blindly roll out their flawed culture change programmes.

What has also become very clear to me is how leaders are themselves becoming the glass ceilings to change, innovation and transformation. And like organizational cultures and teams, the worldview from which a leader operates, can also be mapped alongside the other nested layers.

At the opportunist culture and pseudo team level, leadership is *reactive* and self-serving. It is impulsive and opportunistic.

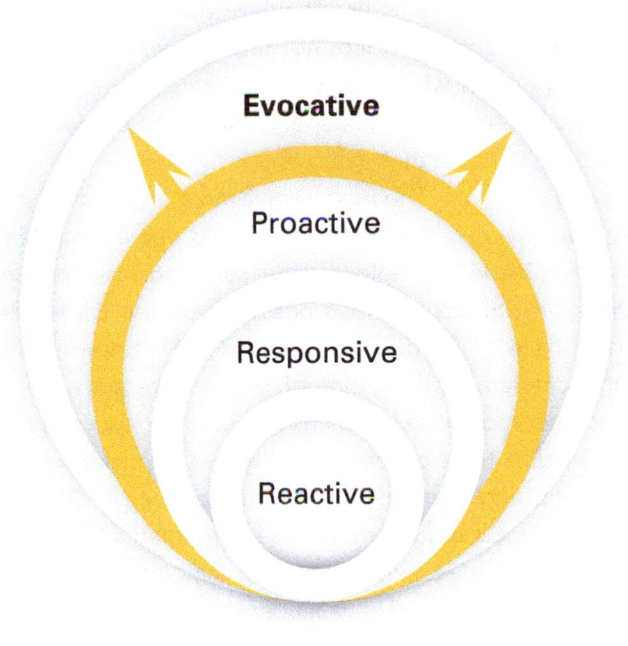

FIGURE 3.9 Leadership layers

Status is part of the mission. Leaders from this layer are typically social butterflies, flitting from one meeting to the next. They desperately want to belong to something successful and be seen to be at the centre of entrepreneurial action. These leaders are often full of energy.

One of the shadow traits of reactive leaders is that they can easily get themselves into trouble by misreading, or missing completely, social cues. They are not particularly good listeners. Well, actually, that's not totally true. They are great at listening out for what they want to hear. They can also fall into angry knee-jerk reactions, and blame others for lack of progress, ie it's never their fault.

Moving swiftly on. The next layer is more *responsive* leadership. This aligns with expert cultures and operational teams. This style of leadership holds a wider set of possible responses to emerging situations. This is possible because leaders from this layer have developed a larger worldview. Knowing more, having more data, working through different scenarios, enables them to offer more measured and appropriate responses.

The shadow traits of responsive leadership include a sense of superiority and even aloofness: 'I know better than you'. They also love a good argument, and see arguments as a natural part of leadership – a way of applying their intellectual horsepower to life and work. These leaders have a tendency to put others down, often having a dig at them through awkward humour. They also seek out evidence to support their existing belief systems.

These leaders are great at managing committees and steering groups, particularly around risk avoidance. Unfortunately, they miss the fact that committees and steering groups should actually be in service of maximizing success, not just minimizing risk. This often creates self-fulfilling loops that increase the likelihood of failure.

Hierarchy is important to the responsive leader. They spend a lot of time looking upwards at the expense of engaging peers, and particularly at the expense of engaging their own people. As mentioned before, they can often fall into a subservient relationship with achiever leaders. Responsive leaders also do everything at their disposal to hide their vulnerabilities. These leaders have typically risen through layers of management because of their expertise, not because of their leadership skills.

Now I am aware that I am being a bit disparaging to these first two layers of leadership. Fortunately for me, and the wider world, the majority of leaders do evolve beyond these two layers and move into *proactive* leadership. This is about setting goals and driving results. These leaders aim high and are single-mindedly focused on delivering on commitments. Proactive leaders are curious to the extent that they are open to anything that will help them deliver their plans better, faster and cheaper. They break problems into manageable parts, solving each piece one at a time. They often have high self-esteem, as success breeds success. They have an intense, personal power about them. They have learnt that motivated people deliver the best results, so they proactively seek out feedback and ways of empowering talent. They dream big and yet have their feet on the ground. They make meaning of their leadership both backwards and forwards in time, ie what they have achieved and what they intend to achieve.

As the proactive leader evolves towards the post-conventional threshold, their capacity to hold larger systems increases. They are usually fast, bright and highly ambitious. They also start to build professional and personal support systems around them – using coaches, mentors and consultants to push and challenge their thinking.

The trap, and a shadow trait of proactive leaders, is their own super-rationality. When things get tough, they believe they will always be able to analyse their way out of it. Unfortunately what came before doesn't always create the blueprint for what comes next – especially in a world where quantum change is the name of the game. When the going gets tough the proactive leader often falls back on two classical weapons of mass destruction. The first is to restructure in order to 'fix business performance'. The second is to dictate behavioural change in order to 'fix their people'. These are responses to the presumption that the organization is simply not performing. All they have to do is increase performance as opposed to face the reality that they might be doing the wrong things.

I remember working with a client who had spent 22 years scaling and replicating the company's founding business model. This had been revolutionary in its day. Two decades on, what had been a unique differentiator was now a core competence of the industry. Aggressively scaling and replicating their original model had brought huge success at the expense of the creativity and strategic capacity of the organization, and of the humanity of its culture. Micro-managing the day-to-day, and obsessing over daily sales, had dehumanized the workplace. I remember one talented, young woman saying how she had taken a few months off on maternity leave. On her return to her open plan office, no one asked her about how she was, how it had gone, or how she was coping with motherhood. She was just a role, not a person. Everyone had their own individual performance targets, and that was all everyone cared about. It was what they were incentivized to care about. This is another shadow trait of proactive leadership – seeing their organization as a machine, and forgetting that it is a living, breathing organism that has feelings and moods, hopes and fears.

Now if the figures are to be believed, 75 per cent of leaders embody responsive or proactive leadership, with 10 per cent stuck in reactive leadership. This means that only 15 per cent transition into the fourth realm. From my experience to date I would argue that this percentage is even smaller. However, the one thing I am clear about is that we need this percentage to increase at speed if we are to innovate our way to more purposeful and sustainable futures and face into the super-wicked problems of our time.

Cultures of innovation and creative teams have one important thing in common. They are both called forward by *evocative* leadership. Evocative leaders love life. They are open to new experiences. They seek meaning and discover purpose. They are able to free themselves from an attachment to the known and an aversion to the unknown. Their attention is positive, open and generative as opposed to defensive, selective and wary. They have an ability to play, and understand that through play we discover ourselves and become more than our selves.

They have the courage and capability to break through social and cultural conventions – determined to realize their highest potential, and inspire others to do the same. They know how to hold a continuous state of readiness or emptiness. This gives them an unimpeded understanding – a wisdom – enabling them to listen deeply to life.

Evocative leaders have developed a quality of consciousness that allows them to access a whole new set of subtle skills. They see potential, appreciate the now and play with reality. They intentionally disturb the status quo in order to release the co-creative potential of organizations. They hold in their being a stillness that allows them to meet the world, moment by moment, in a creative way. They create containers and hold spaces designed to help others surprise themselves with what they can achieve. And, they lead their organizations like the conductor of an orchestra, seeking moments of flow, when the music of innovation bursts forth and puts everyone, inside and outside of the organization into a resonant, co-creative relationship.

One of the shadow traits of evocative leaders is feeling isolated and burdened because others struggle to understand their intentions. This can lead to a gap between them and the next level down that leaves open a vulnerable space in which others can feed misinformation, politics, gossip and rumour, to the detriment of the whole. Ultimately this gap is unsustainable and is only overcome when the leader slows down, deeply listens (with empathy) into this dysfunctional gap, sees and feels into the patterns of thought and action that are getting in the way (including their own), and reawakens the story (or stories) that re-enfold everyone into the future they want to co-create.

The subtle skills of evocative leadership are what this book is really about.

SUMMARY

Before we move on, let me briefly summarize some of the key principles from this chapter:

- Cultures of innovation and creative teams are called forward by evocative leadership.

- Evocative leadership is called forth from a post-conventional worldview.

- Movement from a conventional to post-conventional worldview is the threshold that organizational cultures, teams and leaders need to step over in order to create containers and hold spaces potent enough and large enough to: catalyse creative insight and collective breakthrough; face into the super-wicked problems of our time; and ultimately, evoke the music of innovation – thereby enabling us all to live and work at a higher, co-creative frequency.

- nowhere has developed a simple, four-stage framework of nested layers designed to help organizational cultures, teams and leaders recognize and step over this threshold (Figure 3.10).

- Most cultures become stuck at the achiever stage – the challenge is to move over this threshold and into the fourth realm of the innovator/shaper culture.

- Most teams become stuck in operational and strategic meetings – the challenge is to learn how to move over this threshold into the fourth realm of creative teams.

- Leaders are themselves the glass ceilings for the evolution of cultures and teams, and their development can also be mapped alongside the four-nested levels.

- Less than 15 per cent of leaders evolve into the fourth realm of evocative leadership, and we need this percentage to increase at speed.

Innovator / Shaper
Achiever
Expert
Opportunist

Evolution of cultures

Based on William Torbert and David Rooke et al

Creative
Strategic
Operational
Pseudo

Evolution of teams

Evocative
Proactive
Responsive
Reactive

Evolution of leadership

Based on Gregory Bateson and Roger Benson et al

FIGURE 3.10 A movement over a subtle threshold

HOW THE LOWS
ENABLE THE HIGHS

At the age of 16 I was diagnosed with Crohns Disease. One night, as I was living away from home as part of a summer holiday job working in a café off the south coast of Devon, I awoke with extreme abdominal pains. I was in agony. I tried to roll over and ignore it but I couldn't. The next day I reluctantly went to the doctors believing it would surely go away in time. On my first visit the doctor bizarrely seemed to agree with me. On the second visit, seeing that it was getting worse, he referred me to Plymouth Royal Naval Hospital.

From recollection the Royal Naval Hospital in Plymouth was a tough, strict place; or at least it was to an impressionable teenager. The doctors kept wondering if it was a burst appendix. They chose not to operate, as they weren't sure. What I did know was that I was in extreme pain, my temperature was through the roof, and everyone was really worried.

They chose a course of strong pain relief through drips and other medication and I was soon on the mend. A few weeks later I was out, none the wiser, with an instruction to contact a consultant doctor near my home to explore options going forward.

Three months later I was in the operating theatre having two feet of bowel taken out, for they had found a hole where my appendix used to be (luckily blocked by some fatty tissue – nice!) and that I also had Crohns Disease, an inflammatory bowel disease – and an extreme case thereof.

As you can imagine, this was a life-changing experience for a young person. I subsequently spent a few more times in hospital over the next 15 years whenever I had an attack of the Crohns (not Attack of the Clones a la Star Wars) and found myself having yet more of my colon taken out. Fortunately I have at least 20 feet of colon left.

When I look back on the three most severe periods in hospital, I see them as turning points in my life. Each stint was a low. Trust me, I was down. I'm sure I was not a nice patient to look after. Certainly for the first and second visits I know I had totally lost any sense of perspective.

Yet, all three of these times in hospital were followed by periods of extreme creativity, leading to a quickening of my sense of self and why I was here. It was as if the lows enabled the highs.

04

RIDING THE CREATIVE ROLLERCOASTER

nother way of looking at the four-nested layers is to understand the different biases that each layer has about innovation. For opportunist cultures, innovation is about *ideas*, lots of ideas. For expert cultures, innovation is about turning ideas into *products*. And for achiever cultures, innovation is about the management of innovation as a *process* – maximizing the flow of a pipeline that turns ideas into products and, in turn, gets them successfully to market. This is all great, and all of this is needed.

The discontinuity is that innovator/shaper cultures understand how innovation is born from a *co-creative frequency* – requiring post-conventional containers in which the previous nested layers are brought together in co-creative relationship.

To explain this another way, innovation in opportunist, expert and achiever cultures is based on *horizontal* movement, ie generating ideas and products that are extensions and expansions of the existing paradigm. As you move through the layers, horizontal movement increases in scale due to the greater application of resource and the more efficient and effective leveraging of infrastructure. This horizontal movement is born from an ideation paradigm. The problem with this approach is that innovation is reduced to a numbers game, ie we brainstorm in volume in the hope that we stumble across a few gems. Innovations are therefore forged from accidents. It is important to remember that some of the greatest innovations to transform our world were accidents, eg penicillin, saccharin, microwaves...

For me, ideation is a one-dimensional approach to innovation. Ideas are more often than not generated through the lens of the dominant culture, selected through the lens of the dominant culture, and implemented through the lens of the dominant culture. This endeavour progresses from the lone inventor, through to teams assigned to the research and development of new products, and expands to include marketing and sales – the latter hopefully integrating a deeper understanding of customer wants and needs.

Innovation in the fourth realm, however, is no longer limited to ideation-based activity. Rather, it transitions into an insight-based phenomenon – a *vertical* movement to a meta-position that enables the innovator/shaper to reorder what came before.

This is innovation by design, not by accident. It is based on the post-conventional capacity to catalyse creative insight and collective breakthrough at will and with skill.

As I write this chapter, two creative catalysts from **nowhere** have been holding a four-day PurposeQuest in Patagonia for one of our clients. This process is used to help organizations discover their core purpose – the wellspring from which cultures of innovation are shaped.

It is an intense process. It requires three months of preparation before a team of eight are taken to an isolated venue. In this final deep-dive the core purpose reveals itself in a collective moment of breakthrough. In this particular instance, the

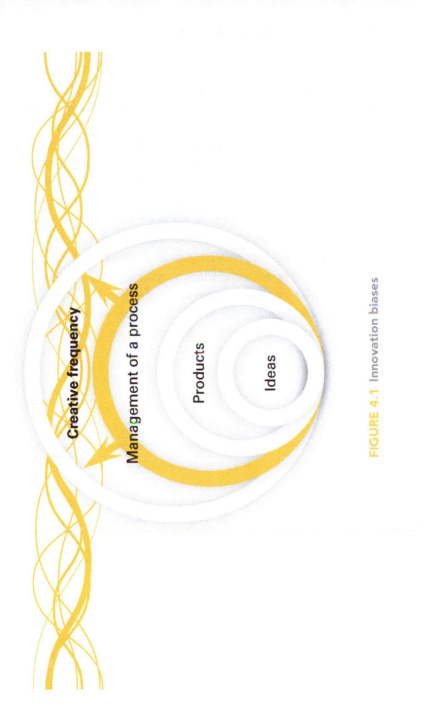

FIGURE 4.1 Innovation biases

sudden vertical movement was anticipated to take place at 3.19 on the afternoon of the fourth and final day. As you would expect, when this prediction was set on the first day everyone thought we were joking. Then as time passes, and we stayed true to our prediction, energy and tension started to increase. When the breakthrough happened one of the team remembered to check the time. It was 3.19 pm.

Now it is not always this precise. It is more common for PurposeQuest teams to experience the final collective breakthrough within 20–30 minutes of our target prediction. I like to think this is not a bad tolerance level in the overall scheme of things. What is more important is that they are not asked to generate their top three options and, subsequently, to choose the best one. Instead, this is about a moment of collective breakthrough where there is a deep and shared knowing that this is their core purpose.

THE SCIENCE OF CREATIVE INSIGHT

While the phenomenon of creative insight feels like it comes from nowhere, it can also be explained, or at least it can at an individual level.

Creative insights unfold through a chain of events in our brains when we have a problem or challenge that logic can't solve. These insights are fleeting and elusive and therefore have historically been hard to study. Yet, scientists around the world are now identifying the neural correlates of creative insight. And, they are showing that we really are thinking differently when we have a creative insight.

Using fMRI and ECG, respectively measuring where and when activities occur in the brain, they have shown that the insight experience begins with a transient dip, or slowing down

FIGURE 4.2 Horizontal ideas vs vertical insights

of activity in our prefrontal lobes, that part of our brain we use to consciously self-monitor ourselves and to manage risk. Taking a new risk, in thought, therefore requires us to turn down, or turn off, this gatekeeper mechanism.

Next there is a burst of alpha waves at the back of our brains, on the right-hand side, that shuts down part of our visual cortex. This in effect allows our brains to blink, cutting off distraction. This is quickly followed, half a second later, by a spike in gamma waves in our anterior superior temporal gyrus, on the right side of our brain, positioned just above our right ear. This is where we experience a flash of insight, and where in an instant we overcome our engrained assumptions and habitual ways of thinking.

This research also shows us that intelligence and creativity are not isomorphic. There are overlaps but they are actually different processes within the brain. So when it comes to creativity and innovation, intelligence is simply overrated.

Scientists now believe that intelligence uses the shorter dendrites or pathways that are more common in the left hemisphere of our brains, compared to the broader branch dendrites in our right hemisphere. These longer, less organized networks gather a broader and more unrelated set of inputs, and therefore associations, allowing a more diverse set of thoughts to meander and collide.

The ability to think in new and novel ways therefore requires us to take risks (by having new experiences and by disrupting our routines), to slow down, to meander and to look inward (to decrease external distractions). Together they alter our cognitive habits, allowing our mind to make new associations.

This research beautifully supports the notion that creativity, and more specifically creative insight, literally occurs when there is a frequency shift in our (alpha and gamma) brainwaves.

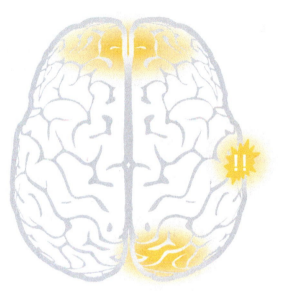

FIGURE 4.3 Neural correlates of creative insights

What is also interesting is that, from our experience of releasing the co-creative potential of teams and organizations, this frequency shift can also be experienced as a collective phenomenon.

THE CREATIVE ROLLERCOASTER

We have spent many years mapping the nature of this co-creative frequency, learning from post-conventional leaders, and de-codifying their conscious and unconscious competences. When we reflect upon the phenomenon of cultures of innovation, creative teams and evocative leadership, and what binds them in symbiosis, we track it back to an ability to ride what we call the creative rollercoaster.

The creative rollercoaster is at one level a *metaphor* for riding the highs and lows of the creative process. At another level it captures the *lived experience* of the fourth realm. At yet another level it is a *map* for designing and catalysing creative insight and collective breakthrough. And, finally, it is the *co-creative frequency* from which the new emerges both into our minds and into the world.

Before I go into more detail about the creative rollercoaster, I'd like to step back and look at some of its foundational constructs.

Theories and concepts of creativity have unfolded over time with multiple facets and different perspectives. The most orthodox of these tend to represent creativity in a series of linear stages. One of the earliest of these was the three-stage model of saturation, incubation and illumination developed by the German physiologist Hermann von Helmholtz. This inspired the development of similar models, culminating with the five-stage model of *first insight*, *saturation*, *incubation*,

FIGURE 4.4 Getzels' five-stage model

illumination and *verification* devised by the American psychologist Jacob Getzels.

These models, although reductionist, are very perceptive. For example, we often have a first insight or notion that there is a problem to solve, an opportunity to grasp or a direction to pursue. This leads into a period where we survey the problem/opportunity space by researching what is already known. Once we have made the known familiar, we sit with the problem/opportunity space to allow new ideas and insights to emerge. It is during this 'mulling over' or incubation period that our unconscious processes take over. As we emerge from this stage, the creative breakthrough or moment of insight is experienced, where new thoughts are brought into the forefront of our consciousness. Finally, this raw data is validated, and further developed (or sometimes thrown out), so that what was a subjective idea can be projected as an objective creation.

To build upon Getzels' model further, creativity is the dance between the *known* and the *unknown*, the conscious and the unconscious, the visible and the invisible, the tangible and the intangible. Creativity is born of this dance or oscillation.

Conventional worldviews focus their attention and belief on the known, conscious, visible and tangible, while postconventional worldviews overtly allow in the unknown, the unconscious, the invisible and the intangible. While I am describing these states linguistically as polarities, they are in fact two sides of the same coin – of our consciousness. Separately, they reflect different complementary aspects of the human experience and together they give a complete Gestalt of our world. Both sides are always in play; it's just that conventional worldviews struggle to make meaning of things that they cannot measure. Post-conventional worldviews, on the other hand, allow that which is currently unknowable in.

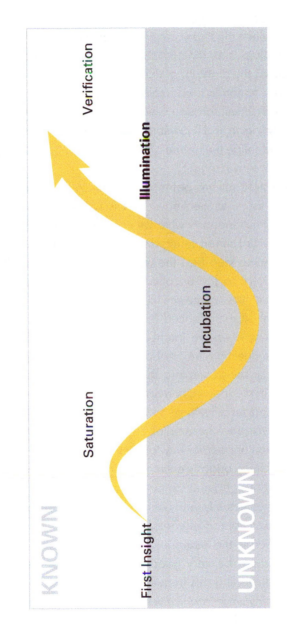

FIGURE 4.5 Getzels' recast

Getzels' model can, therefore, be re-cast to reflect this beautiful dance between the known and the unknown, between that which is conscious and that which is still unconscious. First insight describes the birthing, or making conscious, of a notion or instinct. The notion is then explored and researched using our cognitive faculties, through which we saturate ourselves in what is already known and knowable. During this second phase, we deepen and shape the nature of the problem or opportunity space, and/or we invalidate it.

If the first insight still has potency, we soon come up against the limitations of what we know. This is where we have to acknowledge simultaneously what we know and let go of what we know. This act of surrendering is a post-conventional capacity. It enables us to step into the unknown. This is where the balance shifts back to the unconscious, the invisible and the intangible, as we allow ourselves to incubate our question.

We will have all experienced incubation when we let our minds wander, or when we intentionally stop thinking about a problem or a question we are holding. For some of us this incubation phase transitions into the next phase when we are shaving, or are in the shower, or having a bath. For others it may be when they go for a walk or a run. Whatever our different experiences, these are all examples of 'illuminations', or 'Ahas', when the solution or optimal way forward 'pops' or 'flips' – as if a light is now shining brightly on something that was previously hidden and out of sight, making it now in-sight.

Finally, we intellectually verify our creative in-sight by testing its robustness and appropriateness.

This oscillation is the essence of the creative process. We just happen to also be very good at collapsing the creative process and diminishing this frequency back towards a flatline.

There are many ways in which we do this: the fear of the unknown, being unfamiliar with not-knowing, feeling over-exposed

FIGURE 4.6 A dance between the known and the unknown

and vulnerable, only focusing on the tangible, being overly controlling, emotionally over-reacting, judging others, pushing too hard too quick... and so on. We have been conditioned to flatline, as our educational systems focus almost entirely on the known, at the expense of knowing how to embrace, value and work with the unknown.

AS A METAPHOR

The creative rollercoaster is a metaphor for working with both the known and unknown. We first need a reason, a quest, a question, to get on board, something that we genuinely don't know the answer to and that has potency. Then we need to slow down, change our pace, in order to mine what we know before we let it go and accelerate into the unknown. With enough momentum we can then burst back into the known with 'newness' in our possession.

With practice we can learn to ride ever bigger creative rollercoasters, allowing us to go faster, deeper and higher.

AS A LIVED EXPERIENCE

Personally, I struggle to ride fairground rollercoasters. I have to force myself to participate alongside my family who just love them. As you'll see from the photo below, we all have different emotional responses to letting go. In this instance, mine was to put on a brave face, as I knew the camera was there.

There are of course similarities between riding a real rollercoaster and riding the creative rollercoaster. For me, riding a real rollercoaster starts with questions: Do I want to do this? Have I the courage to do this? Is there a good enough reason to do this?

FIGURE 4.7 Emotional responses to riding
the creative rollercoaster

Once I'm strapped in my mind starts to question why I am doing this. I would have been quite happy to watch rather than participate.

Then comes the slow beginning as we are ratcheted up to the top of the first crest. The anticipation builds until the release, when we start hurtling down into the abyss.

I now know I have a choice. I can either fight it all the way, shut my eyes and hold on for dear life, desperate for it to end; or, I can trust the process, let go, go with the flow, and see and feel things that I never experienced before.

The lived experience of riding the creative rollercoaster begins by on-boarding people to the challenge, to the quest, to the reason to get aboard. This should not be rushed.

Next comes the ratcheting-up stage where we each share what we already know. We get everything on the table, and more, as we saturate ourselves with knowledge, share our expertise, and allow the power of our intellect to take us as far as it can go. Then we reach the tipping point. We can't go any further doing what we have always done. We have to let go and accelerate into the unknown.

Every time we take a team through this process we introduce them to a drawing of the creative rollercoaster as part of their on-boarding. I think when they hear it for the first time, they go: 'Oh, more consultant speak!' When they find themselves, hours later, experiencing the bottom of the creative rollercoaster, they intuitively take some level of comfort that this is where they are supposed to be, and that it is a vital part of the process. This may be little comfort, yet it is often just enough for them to stay with it, to trust the process, and to earn the breakthrough they seek.

AS A MAP

The creative rollercoaster is also a map to help us design and catalyse creative insight and collective breakthrough. Let me elaborate.

The double exclamation marks (!!) at the end of the creative rollercoaster are what we design to. They represent a twin breakthrough. The first exclamation mark represents the *innovative output* that needs to be generated, whether that is a new product, service, solution, process, strategy or pathway. Sometimes it needs to be a relational breakthrough between key leaders or stakeholders, which if shifted would unleash exponential value in a team, or across a function or organization, or across multiple organizations. What is important is this innovative output is tangible, objective and measurable. It is generated by the team, yet is other than the team, in that it has inherent value in and of itself.

The second exclamation mark represents the *transformational outcome*, ie we have changed through the process of having the breakthrough. We can no longer go back and see the world or each other in the same way again. The way we make meaning of our work, of the world, and even of ourselves, has reordered. We have glimpsed the fourth realm and our belief systems have subtly altered. The world might not be what we thought it was, and an opening is now in process.

The beauty of the double exclamation marks is that creative teams generate innovative outputs while also integrating enough of the meta-perspective from which they generated the outputs to enable and resource them to help on-board others into the implementation phase. This minimizes the 'lost in translation' effect, where the value and impact of something new and different is diluted because of how it is viewed and understood by the existing dominant culture and its normalized frames of reference.

The double-exclamation marks are the Holy Grail we are looking for when we ride the creative rollercoaster. Evocative leaders use the creative rollercoaster to design creative interventions and journeys that generate breakthrough. Of course, with experience, they get to know what type, level and depth of breakthrough is achievable in certain time frames. For example, in my own context, I don't know a quicker way of generating the collective breakthrough needed in a Purpose-Quest in less than four days. I'm open to the challenge but not stupid enough to commit to it. Similarly, I know how to generate breakthrough insights into critical business projects in three days, or generate value-chain innovation with multiple companies in two days. And, that a breakthrough strategy for a global corporation, which is a complex choreography of co-creative interventions, will take around six to nine months for the final pattern to reveal itself.

Whatever the timeline, and the challenge, the creative rollercoaster holds the coherence of the design. The bigger the creative challenge the more time we need to put into the on-boarding phase. This includes ensuring that the break-through questions that we are questing into have enough energy, sponsorship and strategic context to literally 'hold' a diverse group of people on the creative rollercoaster for long enough. The *breakthrough questions* needs to generate enough traction and down-force.

Next come the *three carriages*. The first is about building the *container*. Choosing the right people, freeing them up for the right amount of time, finding the right physical spaces and places in which to hold the work, on-boarding the team to the breakthrough questions, to the strategic imperative, to each other, and to what they already know.

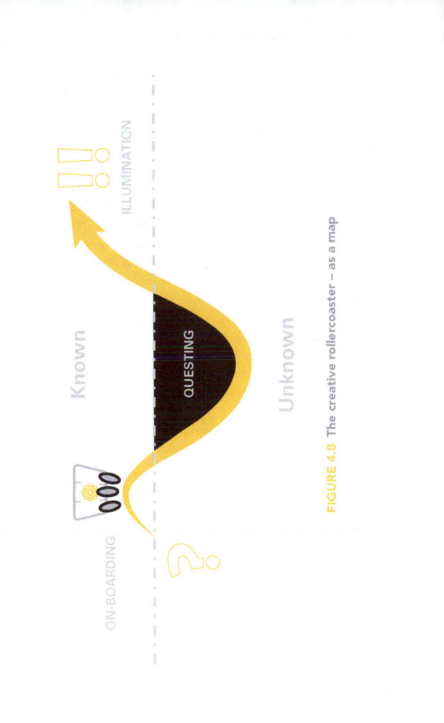

FIGURE 4.8 The creative rollercoaster – as a map

The second carriage refers to our *self-awareness*. In the fourth realm, subject and object are intimately interconnected. How I am determines how well I (and therefore we) ride the highs and lows of the creative process. It is all too easy to collapse the process, taking me and us towards a flatline experience. Raising everyone's self-awareness always ups the chance of success.

The third carriage takes this even further. It refers to our *relational* and our *systemic awareness*. We are all defined by our relationships and our interdependences, whether we know it or not. How we are in relationship, and how we pay attention to wider systems at play, will either enhance or diminish our collective ability to ride the creative rollercoaster. All it takes is one dysfunctional relationship across a team to leak (value) and we increase the chance of collapsing the creative tension needed for a vertical movement and a collective breakthrough. So deepening the quality of relationships within and across a team is another vital ingredient for resourcing us to step into the unknown.

The design challenge is therefore to pay attention to these three carriages just enough to support the nature and type of breakthrough that is needed. There is no indulgence to this on-boarding. And yet, the correlation is profound. The challenge is to *on-board* a team to the extent that it is necessary to achieve breakthrough. Miss this part out, and the team will by default, not necessarily by intent, collapse the creative rollercoaster when the going gets tough. They will then blame the leader and in turn the process, as they have separated themselves from both.

Leaning into the emerging future / Finding and following flow

FIGURE 4.9 The creative rollercoaster – as a frequency

AS A CO-CREATIVE FREQUENCY

In its highest form, the creative rollercoaster describes a co-creative frequency, a resonance and a tone, that emerges from post-conventional containers and spaces designed to evoke the music of innovation.

This frequency is more specifically a dance between the *explicate* order (that which is unfolded, independent and distinguished) and the *implicate* order (that which is still enfolded, interdependent and undistinguished). The challenge is to lean into the emerging future, into the implicate, more regularly and more frequently, and to find and follow flow. Leaning into the emerging future, and finding and following flow, requires a new and next generation of subtle skills. One of these skill-sets we call 'de-veiling skills'. These include:

Learning to slow down and lean back

As we move into the unknown, we need to learn to slow down time. The unknown is not linear, so we have to see and work with data differently. We need to change our approach and our pace, by leaning back – literally. I sometimes have to move leaders back in their chairs physically so they become more receptive and less on guard, opening a space for the new.

Deepening the quality of contact

As the creative tension increases so we need intentionally to thicken the space between people. This thickening primes the field for the 'new' to reveal itself. This thickening happens as a result of people disclosing more, speaking their truth more, exploring the nature of the space between each other more. We follow a simple rule: create a safe space, and then a healthy space, if you want a co-creative space to emerge. It is only from a place of trust that we can leap.

Feeling into the wider context

As our intellect can only take us so far, we need to tune into other ways of knowing. These include gathering data from our feelings, our bodies and our intuitions. With practice, we can start to feel into a wider context and its underlying and inter-related rhythms and cycles. That which we previously thought to be isolated and separate is often the opposite, woven into the fabric of cost and consequence.

Handing over knowing to our collective intelligence

At some point we stop trying to solve 'it' ourselves, and realize that innovation happens at new and novel intersections. We surrender to this collective endeavour and realize that each of us holds a different part of the puzzle. Moreover, when we each slow down, lean back, deepen our quality of contact, and feel into the wider context, we start to tap into a collective intelligence beyond that which is in the room. We start to tap into a wider knowing field.

Sharing observations

When this happens we need to stay present and notice what is, for newness is momentary and fragile. It is so easy to miss. The challenge is to catch the sparks and to mine the cracks by sharing and exploring what we see and feel in real time.

Sitting with 'not knowing'

We also need to be comfortable with 'not knowing', being careful not to fill the empty space with our ego or our impatience. While we can take comfort in what we know, the challenge is to stay empty and create a vacuum that pulls the new into being. It's counter-intuitive. We need to draw our bow back into the unknown before we can propel the arrow forward into the known.

Bracketing

One of the things that get in the way of the unknown is 'us' – our needs, desires, wants, fears, biases and filters. So we need to bracket our agenda and take ourselves out of the equation.

Equalizing

And, we need to try to hold a beginner's mind, a state of equalization, enabling us to witness what is arising in the space between, feeling into what needs to take more form, and what needs to take less form.

Languaging

Lastly, we need to help the new come into the world. How we language it into being can be make or break. By using story and narrative we can draw people gradually into a new frame of reference, or we can jolt then into a new frame of reference. Either way, we need to use language to pull the future into the present.

SUMMARY

This chapter has been about the frequency shifts that take place in creative teams and across cultures of innovation. We touched on how:

- Ideation is a one-dimensional approach to innovation, as ideas are more often than not generated through the lens of the dominant culture, selected through the lens of the dominant culture, and implemented through the lens of the dominant culture.

- Innovation in the fourth realm transitions into an insight-based phenomenon – a vertical movement to a meta-position that enables the innovator-shaper to reorder that which came before.

- Innovation in the fourth realm is by design, and is based on the post-conventional capacity to catalyse creative insight and collective breakthrough at will and with skill.

- Scientists have now discovered the neural correlates of creative insight and how insight is born from a frequency shift in (alpha and gamma) brainwaves.

- The phenomenon of cultures of innovation, creative teams and evocative leadership are bound in symbiosis by their ability to ride what we call the 'creative rollercoaster'.

- The creative rollercoaster is first and foremost a metaphor for working with both the known and unknown.

- Second, it describes a lived experience of riding the highs and lows of the creative process.

- Third, it can be used as a map to help us design and catalyse creative insight and collective breakthrough.

- And fourth, it is a co-creative frequency, a resonance and a tone, that emerges from post-conventional containers and spaces designed to evoke the music of innovation.

- Lastly, we began to introduce the need for a new and next generation of subtle skills to help us lean into the emerging future and find and follow flow.

In the next chapter I would like to introduce eight things that become available to organizations once they have learned to step over this golden threshold and play in and with the fourth realm.

THE CREATIVE POWER OF DISBELIEF

When I was a doctoral student I had to undertake a certain number of teaching hours with undergraduates. I chose to teach life drawing in the art department as five or six years earlier I'd had a life-changing experience with a Japanese (master) teacher. He had forced us to use our unfamiliar hand. He got us to draw things upside-down, back-to-front, to music, in silence, against the clock... anything and everything to confound orthodoxy, interrupt the ego and disturb the status quo.

Using the drawing techniques that I had learned from my teacher, and subsequently from the work of Betty Edwards and her famous book *Drawing on the Right Side of the Brain* (1979), I came to understand and develop other methodologies that made the familiar unfamiliar and the unfamiliar familiar. I became fascinated with how, in a very short period of time, you could help novice drawers draw something that they never thought they could. They would come in with a belief that they were 'no good at drawing'; and yet in 40 minutes, through a series of eight five-minute drawings, you could transform their belief system, through the creative power of disbelief, where they would end up saying, 'I can't believe I just did that'.

This was a foundational insight for me, that learning through peak experience can reorder our sense of self, and our sense of the world around us. By intervening at this level, the world seemed magical again.

FIGURE 5.1 Drawings

FIGURE 5.1 Continued

05

WHAT AWAITS US ON THE OTHER SIDE?

The impetus for organizations of all kinds to learn how to step over this subtle threshold continues to grow. We need to embrace diversity and leverage difference in order to innovate our way to more purposeful and sustainable futures. We need to break through the numerous super-wicked problems of our time if we are to create futures fit for generations to come. We need a new and next generation of leaders to step forward who can work from the fourth realm. And we need these leaders to evoke the music of innovation within their organizations and across wider and more complex ecologies of resource.

The challenge for evocative leaders is to create and hold post-conventional containers and spaces in which teams and organizations can ride the highs and lows of the creative process, work with creative tension, tap into our collective intelligence and thereby discover the new, by design. This is in contrast to teams and organizations that consciously, unconsciously and prematurely collapse creative tension, avoid conflict and don't speak their truth. Or where it is unsafe to challenge the status quo, show vulnerability and be seen to not know.

Part of the challenge derives from the fact that we naturally resist taking leaps of faith. It can take senior leaders weeks, months and even years to take a leap of faith and experiment with new ways of working. They, of course, need to build up the courage, conviction and evidence to do so. When they do take even a mini-leap of faith, they almost immediately regret not having done so sooner.

It isn't uncommon to hear the words: 'We weren't ready to do this two years ago, the conditions weren't right then.' This is sometimes true, but often not. The reality is their conservatism and habitual patterns have led them to being even further behind the curve. As the saying goes, 'The work that gets in the way of the work is the work'.

I can also appreciate how difficult it is to let go of that which had previously made us successful. Leading ourselves and others into the unknown is at first glance a mad thing to do. It is also the most important thing to do if we want to be true shapers of the future.

In light of some of our experiments to date in helping leaders, teams and organizations step over this subtle threshold we have caught exciting glimpses of what awaits organizations on the other side. To this effect, I would like to outline eight value-creating and value-capturing capacities that become more available to post-conventional leaders, teams and organizations when they step over into the fourth realm. I have already outlined the first three, and yet, let me add a little more texture and colour to each of them.

1. CULTURES OF INNOVATION

Cultures of innovation are shaped by evocative leaders and sometimes by evocative leadership teams. They allow the

FIGURE 5.2 Cultures of innovation

unknown, the unconscious, the invisible and the intangible to become part of the way things are. They recognize that innovation is the co-creative dance between the explicate and the implicate, and that creativity is the co-creative dance between the known and the unknown. They also understand that creativity is not born from a blank sheet of paper, rather it is evoked through the use of liberating-disciplines. These liberating-disciplines hold us in a coherent pattern, while inviting us to continually re-order how we make meaning of our work, and the world around us. They support and challenge us to ride the highs and lows of the creative process. And, they interrupt the distorted behaviours of opportunist, expert and achiever cultures that by default collapse the creative roller-coaster back to a flatline.

It is also important to remember that cultures of innovation weave achievers, experts and opportunists into a coherent, co-creative community. These are all critical roles and contributions. Cultures of innovation challenge us to create unity in diversity, optimizing relationships such that we surprise and delight one another. This is a result of the culture being able to see, value and leverage difference, as opposed to judging one another through the lens of our own respective worldviews.

Cultures of innovation are also founded, nourished and bound by a core purpose. They feel part of an unfolding story and a pattern of shared endeavours that really matter. They are dynamic in their structure in that they use structure to both define difference and to put difference into a co-creative relationship.

Innovation is no longer a one-dimensional activity. Idea-jamming, product development and the management of innovation pipelines all have their place, and are held within a creative climate and cultural container that by design doesn't allow the ego, the known, the analytical, and the power of our intellects to overly dominate. While these elements are all valued, they are held in a dynamic imbalance with other ways of knowing, being and becoming.

This in turn demands greater choice-fulness, as more is now available in the moment. How people meet, how they relate, how decisions are made become more complex and also more potent. There is no desire to suppress this complexity as they have learned to create containers and hold spaces in which complexity re-patterns and chaos reorders. The challenge is to hold these spaces strongly enough and for long enough.

Opportunities, experts, achievers and shapers all come alive within this post-conventional container as it holds them in their rightful place, exchanging fair value, while feeling part of something bigger.

These cultures are rare, yet fortunately less rare than ever before. Myth and story build up around these cultures, for it is so difficult to put your finger on why they are so magical. This is because cultures of innovation also use stories to subtly shape the future.

2. CREATIVE TEAMS

As I've outlined before, creative teams are the DNA of cultures of innovation. They form around quests and questions. Their purpose is to ride the highs and lows of the creative process, of the creative rollercoaster, and to illuminate new insight.

We can only ride this creative rollercoaster if we surrender to it. And, it is in surrendering to it that our frequency shifts, and our ability to dance and oscillate between the known and unknown, the conscious and the unconscious, the explicate and the implicate, increases.

With practice we can get better at riding the creative rollercoaster.

Creative teams understand that inputs are only potential clues rather than truths. They relish difference and juxtaposition, for this generates creative tension and starts to describe the empty space between. They have the courage and skill to hold this creative tension rather than collapse it, maximizing the chance that a vertical movement will take place.

The problem with this picture is that most organizations don't know how to do this. Some would espouse that they do with rapid action teams (RAT) or skunk teams. To be fair, these teams can echo some of the characteristics of creative teams but they mostly still rely on brainpower rather than creativity.

An IBM Survey in 2010 with 1,500 CEOs in the United States identified that the number one quality these leaders wanted and needed to develop to remain competitive was creativity. A recent article in *The Wall Street Journal*, 'In Search of the Spark ... and the Next Big Thing' (Bussey, 2013), describes how 'Innovation is the fuel of economic growth and is the Holy Grail for companies and countries alike around the world'. It also postulates: 'What will happen when India and China finally learn the magic sauce of innovation in bulk?'

The challenge is that the secret sauce is not in my mind the conscious, linear competences that are normally espoused. For example, following the rules of brainstorming, or learning design thinking, are useful. These methodologies are great at optimizing horizontal opportunities. Yet, they are simply not in the same ballpark as learning to ride the creative rollercoaster and tapping into our collective intelligence.

When creativity becomes a collective phenomenon, magic happens. We don't have to look any further than the animated film company Pixar to see this exemplified. The trouble with

FIGURE 5.3 Creative teams

this example is that they were founded upon this premise, they are campus based, and their founders are still holding the container and thereby optimizing the frequency at which their organization operates. The challenge for most organizations and cabinet governments is how to evolve and transform to this frequency from a legacy state.

It is also important not to confuse creative teams with creative agencies, where in effect you rent creativity. 'Creativity' within this context is about branding, design, media and advertising, which are all still based on linear methodologies of taking and shaping a brief, undertaking contextual and anthropological research (including dare I say it 'focus groups'), brainstorming alternatives, working up the best two or three options (even though they know the one they want it to be) and presenting them back to the client.

There's obviously a great business in this. As ever, the real genius behind their preferred idea will have happened by accident, not by design, and will have been generated by one or two talented individuals on the team.

Michael Wolff, one of the co-founders of world-renowned branding agency Wolff Olins, and one of the grand-daddies of branding, recently shared his belief with me that great branding ideas emerge in an instant and when you least expect it. He laughs when he then goes on to say how the challenge is to design a profitable business model around this truism, as opposed to hiding it within an industry of activity that doesn't really add much value.

To go back to the thought – What will happen when India and China finally learn the secret sauce of innovation in bulk? – I hope these and other so-called emerging economies have the courage to explore creativity and innovation as a collective activity and not a lone one. If they do, it would be like passing analogue and leaping straight to digital.

To put it simply, tapping into collective intelligence begins with the power of creative teams.

3. EVOCATIVE LEADERSHIP

Evocative leaders are those who call forth cultures of innovation and creative teams. They literally draw them out of us. Evocative leaders are shapers and makers. They want to change the world. They don't just do this by setting big, hairy, audacious goals. Instead, they create containers and hold spaces in which we can surprise ourselves with what we can achieve. They enfold us into something bigger. They write us into compelling stories, and with a true emergent spirit, they challenge us to co-author the next chapters.

To create and hold these post-conventional containers, evocative leaders develop two key abilities. The first is what we call *voltage* – the ability to work with and hold the potential difference between the highs and lows of the creative process. The greater a leader's voltage, the greater the highs (of knowing) and the deeper the lows (of not-knowing) they can ride. This is vital, for too often leaders collapse the creative rollercoaster because they struggle to not-know, and worry about being seen to not-know. Moreover, voltage also refers to an ability to oscillate between the known and the unknown, and between the explicate and the implicate, at will and with skill.

The second ability is what we call *capacity*. This is the capacity to be bigger than the greatest disturbance in the room or system. Evocative leadership is about intentionally disturbing systems in order to release their co-creative potential. And in times of disturbance it is important leaders don't get knocked off their centre. It's very difficult to generate the centripetal force necessary to keep themselves, let alone others, on the creative rollercoaster. To this effect, it is vital that leaders hold a state of equanimity in the face of the disturbance. (Please note I use the terms voltage and capacity more metaphorically than literally.)

Evocative leaders are therefore magicians. They use both their voltage and capacity to create containers and hold spaces in which achievers, experts and opportunists can make music together. I will outline some of the subtle skills of evocative leadership in the next chapter.

4. BREAKTHROUGH STRATEGY

About five years ago one of our clients said to us: 'You have helped transform our leaders, shifted our culture and reshaped our global brand. Through the innovation work we have undertaken together we have been catching glimpses of more co-creative futures. Could you apply this approach to strategy?'

What we developed from this creative challenge we now call 'breakthrough strategy'. It is now about 50 per cent of our total work.

For decades we have seen how, as the saying goes, 'culture eats strategy for breakfast, every day'. For us, this refers to how strategies get lost in translation, as they are only seen and understood through ingrained cultural filters. It also refers to how most strategies are born out of the dominant culture, and in so doing replicate their self-limiting beliefs and patterns. Strategy and culture do not equate to the hard and soft sides of business respectively. They are two sides of the same coin. I believe they are inextricably linked.

Companies are used to paying enormous amounts of money on strategy, often because there aren't enough strategic smarts and manpower within their own organizations. Meanwhile, they

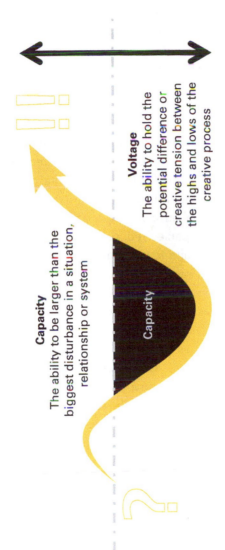

Capacity
The ability to be larger than the biggest disturbance in a situation, relationship or system

Voltage
The ability to hold the potential difference or creative tension between the highs and lows of the creative process

Capacity

FIGURE 5.4 Evocative Leadership

take culture for granted and dismiss it because it is intangible, un-macho, subtle and difficult.

Developing a new strategy can take days, weeks and months. Shaping and embedding a humming culture takes years. The latter is way more difficult. The irony is that cultures of innovation are the only source of true and sustainable competitive advantage.

Breakthrough strategies, therefore, emerge from an ecology of creative teams and are brought to life through cultures of innovation. But before I offer a few more glimpses, let's momentarily review the history of strategy.

Strategy as a formal business tool is only about 50 years old, born of helping companies reduce and manage costs, focus on consumers and understand the competitive landscape. These '3Cs' evolved into the '3Ps' – positioning, processes and people – leading in turn to the two main strategic schools of thought: strategy as positioning and strategy as organizational learning.

By the late Nineties those that had integrated this knowledge saw everyone else start to catch up. Over time, these strategic competencies became table stakes rather than differentiators, and this is why we see the same strategic frameworks across the majority of global corporations.

Strategy is in large part about leveraging an organization's unique differentiators so as to out-innovate the competition. And innovation is, as I have outlined before, more than an intellectual activity and more than the management of a process.

Strategy itself needs to be an innovative activity. Having loads of 'smarts' in a room crafting strategy off-line can add value, but it bypasses the subtle and more imaginative aspects of what strategy (and culture) can be.

Another trap that I've already mentioned is to confuse strategy with strategic planning. Strategic planning is useful for gaining bottom-up data to help make tough decisions about the allocation of finite budget and resource and to track implementation. This is not strategy. Strategy by numbers is not strategy. Numbers are important but numbers should only top and tail a strategy, ie what we are aiming for, and how we test and validate our assumptions.

Some of my current preferred quotes about great strategy are from Richard Rumelt who wrote *Good Strategy/Bad Strategy* (2011):

> *'A good strategy doesn't just draw on existing strengths, but creates strength through the coherence of its design.'*

> *'An insightful reframing of the current situation can create whole new patterns of advantage.'*

Breakthrough strategy is the imaginative reframing of the future, and how to shape that future, in ways that identify innovative patterns of advantage, and then embed and embody this wisdom in dynamic 'frameworks' that enable us to hold both planned and emergent activities in creative tension through the coherence of their designs.

Breakthrough strategies use core purpose as their energetic wellspring. They are formed from a worldview shift and because of this shift. Their strength is based on great analysis of the known and the creative exploration of the unknown. And they turn volatility, uncertainty, complexity and ambiguity into strategic opportunities and assets for growth.

TABLE 5.1 Breakthrough strategy

Expert strategy	Breakthrough strategy
An expert model	A questing model
Analysis and fact-driven	Worldview and pattern-shift
Telling and selling	Priming and repatterning
Planned and objective work	Emergent and subjective work
Linear value chains	Ecologies of innovation and resource
Top-down and/or bottom-up	Co-created & spread virally through core energy
Fragmented and political	Leveraging diversity and creative tension

In the fourth realm, strategy is a relational and spatial activity. Our capacity to wander with wonder into the unknown is dependent on our self, relational and systemic awareness. Our ability to see new insight, and then to pattern and sequence those insights into the most elegant pathways for moving forward, is a spatial activity.

Breakthrough strategy is also a lived phenomenon and not a deck of PPT slides. It is designed to hold a deeper wisdom that cuts through organizational resistance and inertia, while amplifying organizational curiosity and creativity.

FIGURE 5.5 Breakthrough strategy

5. ECOSYSTEM INNOVATION

Embracing diversity, leveraging new and novel intersections and exploring the space between are the lifeblood of creativity and innovation. Riding the creative rollercoaster is the blueprint. Creating containers and holding spaces enable us collectively to get on-board the creative rollercoaster, and keeps us on the rails as the creative tension and momentum builds.

These containers start from within, with the internal voltage and capacity to walk through life as a creative adventure. As our voltage and capacity increase so does the size and potency of the container we can create and the spaces we can hold.

With practice these containers and spaces can expand to hold teams, functions and whole organizations on the creative rollercoaster. Or, at least, you now have a choice to ride it and don't need to flatline by default.

The size of the Co-Creative Container (CC)
= Voltage (V) × Capacity (C)

Some leaders develop their voltage and capacity to the extent that they are able to create containers and hold spaces beyond the boundaries of their organizations, and therefore beyond their hierarchical control. This is when it gets even more interesting. This is when leaders hold spaces for ecosystem innovation.

Ecosystem innovation is when organizations from a current and/or future value chain, or ecosystem, get together to innovate by generating creative insights and collective breakthroughs in the space between.

Ecosystem innovation enables organizations to move beyond transactional relationships and into creative partnerships. It is based on trust, passion and shared risk. And it requires all parties to take a leap of faith in order to shape the new.

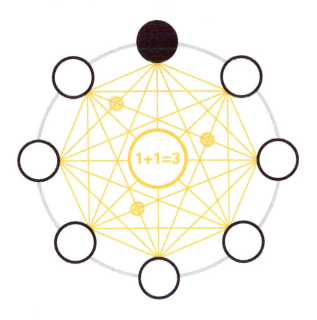

FIGURE 5.6 Ecosystem innovation

I'd like to share a couple of high-level examples. I remember that as part of a creative partnership with one of our long-term global clients, our work was to design the annual conference for their top 200 leaders. After four consecutive years of designing and catalysing these three-day interventions, the CEO challenged us to get even bolder. To cut a long story short, we proposed taking these conferences regional, significantly increasing the size of them to around 400 leaders in each region, and inviting and including throughout the three days key leaders and stakeholders from their wider ecosystem of suppliers, distributors, regulators, customers...

Going regional and increasing the number of people was challenging enough on time, energy and budget. To allow 'externals' into their closed sessions was just madness.

Six months later we were running the first one of these co-creative conferences in North America. One of the executive team, who had been adamant that this was a stupid and risky idea, came over to me at the end of the first day and said, 'Today has been truly amazing'.

Now this was not as simple as a stakeholder-engagement session. We had spent four years helping these executive leaders build a culture of innovation, learn how to use the power of creative teams, and develop a portfolio of micro-skills for riding the highs and lows of the creative process. They were able to create containers and hold spaces in which their guests could come into community with them, and join them aboard the creative rollercoaster. By the end of the second day the 'guests' were discovering things about the company that they didn't know, and were co-creating new business opportunities. The guests also started to find co-creative opportunities in the space between. It was amazing to see. The level of appreciation was immense.

This shared peak experience fundamentally reshaped a large number of business relationships, and was repeated as we took this 'event' to five other regions around the world. Five years later they continue to generate new value through these creative partnerships, and have learned to expand the container even further.

Another manifestation of ecosystem innovation is when a number of companies in a shared value chain or ecosystem come together to generate innovative solutions around a breakthrough question – a question that they each have a vested interest in, a passion for, and that is strategically important enough to give up a few days of their time.

In this instance one of the companies needs to step forward to initiate the possibility. While these companies are coming together to generate tangible, innovative outputs that they can then go and execute, the real win is what happens when they have a shared experience of collective breakthrough. Something reorders in their relationship. They start to see each other differently. They move from transactional relationships to creative partnerships, often leading to exponentially greater value-creation and value-capture opportunities that neither party could have previously foreseen.

6. LEADING THE HUMAN DIMENSIONS OF CHANGE

Another capability that opens up as we step over the threshold into the fourth realm is how to lead people through the human dimensions of change while undertaking large business process re-engineering programmes. Whether it's outsourcing, insourcing, off-shoring, building shared service centres, building a new manufacturing plant... the main focus quite rightly needs to be on the technical aspects of change (design and build) and then on programme management. The only problem with this is that the human dimensions of change are only given a token, one-dimensional nod with a stream dedicated to 'change management', ie stakeholder engagement and communications.

It's common knowledge that a significant proportion of large-scale change programmes fail as a result of the organizational system defending, both consciously and unconsciously, the status quo. For example, there are many examples of large business process re-engineering programmes that have been pushed into organizations, only for shadow business processes – the old way things were done – to spring back up. This totally undermines the time, money and energy put into the programme, wastes tens if not hundreds of millions of dollars' worth of investment, and generates a lack of faith in top management.

It's important to remember that organizations are first and foremost human systems. Mad to have to even say. Human beings don't mind change, they just don't like *being* changed. Most change programmes forget this. This is where working from the post-conventional realm can optimize the chance of success of these types of programmes, and thereby minimize the very real cost of organizational resistance.

These types of programmes are by nature complex. The tendency of experts and achievers when confronted with complexity is to break it into manageable parts and to design fragmented solutions. At one level this is practical and sensible. The danger is losing the sense of the whole. Each part might look beautiful – ie well designed in isolation – yet when things need to be reassembled back into a whole, the parts often don't fit.

Two things are happening. First is the tendency of achiever leaders to push and push, in order to demonstrate their prowess.

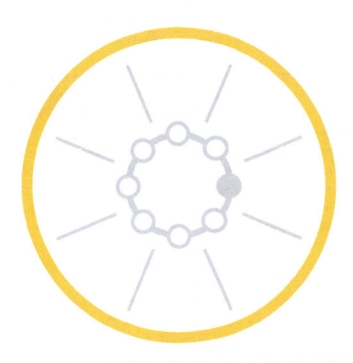

FIGURE 5.7 Leading the human dimensions of change

Fast and independent is their style. Second is how designs are often created in a vacuum. What I mean by this is the design might look good on paper but will often lack wisdom. Too many times I've seen new 'designs' for business processes, or even marketing processes, being created at the centre, from HQ, without listening and integrating the wisdom and experience of the people whose job it has been, and will continue to be, to manage and deliver these processes. The arrogance of it is astounding.

This is also a costly affair. I know of one client who had to scrap $13 million-worth of system and process designs simply because they hadn't talked to colleagues in IT. What they had designed on paper simply wasn't possible in reality.

These large-scale change programmes also by default displace people, create redundancies, and require the establishment of new communities and functions. In so doing people's sense of belonging is disrupted, as is their sense of place. This is what generates organizational resistance. Moreover, if these changes are positioned in such a way that they make the previous structures and processes 'wrong', then this disrespect of what came before multiplies this resistance.

Post-conventional leaders and teams are able to work with complexity and are able to lead people through the human dimensions of change. Leaders first need to know how to inspire, to paint a picture of a better future we can all move towards. Next, leaders need to compassionately speak the truth to name why the status quo is not good enough. Leaders often fudge this part, and fall back into convincing mode. Compassionately speaking the truth enables people to let go of the past and the present so they can then allow something new in. If this is done well, there is then a natural mourning and an emotional outpouring. This is all part of change. The trap here is for leaders to over-protect their people from the pain of change, rather than support them through it. This is the time for leaders to stop talking and to start listening. When you give your people a damned good listening to, they start to feel heard, they begin to open, and they move to becoming part of the solution. In short, the creative rollercoaster is also an emotional rollercoaster.

I'd like to add one further dimension to these types of change initiatives, to highlight a further need for post-conventional containers. Let me animate it through the example of outsourcing or the creation of shared service centres. These programmes are mostly about generating efficiencies across operational processes and systems, especially when global organizations discover they have tens, if not hundreds, of ways in which they process invoices, deal with expenses, manage payroll... or how they endlessly customize a myriad of IT systems. Simplifying to a global process means people need to let go and surrender to being part of something bigger. Whether this is about HR processes, or IT processes, or procurement or finance processes, or all of the above, if they are to be outsourced, the biggest challenge isn't the community of 'operators' that are being displaced, moved, or made redundant. Of course you want and need to support these populations with due care and attention. Instead, the most challenging populations are those whose core identity now has to change. For example, HR business partners, who were previously responsible for day-to-day hygiene and lifecycle processes, lose a large part of what made up their everyday identity as a service function. This means the function itself, in this instance HR, needs to transform its core identity from within – eg from a service function to an insight function. These types of functions don't like change on this scale. They often either go into denial about it, and/or come out fighting in an effort, once again, to complicate the landscape by creating exceptions to the new rules.

This is where executive steering groups need to hold a post-conventional mindset. When they 'steer' large-scale change, they need to monitor technical progress and live budgets while also raising their awareness to the costs and consequences of change on their people's sense of belonging, place and identity. This is where change becomes an elegant choreography and where organizational resistance is minimized. This also means holding executive sponsors and leaders in their own creative tension, as their own sense of identity, and therefore power bases, need to transform too. You can normally track back cultural resistance to power plays at the top of organizations.

7. NEXT GENERATION COMMUNICATIONS, BRANDING AND 'DE-SIGN'

In light of all of the above, and in the context of my own roots, it would be remiss of me not to come full circle and explore how design (or de-sign) morphs as we step over this threshold. Before I do, let me also share some brief thoughts on communications and branding.

Playing with how we make meaning is one of the core characteristics of the fourth realm. In this context communication is another way of tuning frequency. This means seeing communication as more than messaging to seeing communication as a catalyst of 'outcome'. What I mean by this is that leadership is the act of leading people on a journey, and in today's world that journey is far from black and white. There are times when

FIGURE 5.8 Next generation de-sign

leaders need to inspire, or need to disrupt, or need to deepen contact, or need to weave... Designing communications that support and shape the different energetic needs of the people at different times on a journey is far more productive and impactful than focusing on messaging. Success is to affect both.

Meanwhile, the nature of corporate branding also shifts in the fourth realm. The cosmetic application of a corporate identity alongside a clever strapline just doesn't cut it. Branding is itself an act of followership, designed to create allegiance, loyalty and community, while also building equity and reputation. And from the fourth realm branding enables people to feel a part of something that matters. A post-conventional brand should sync the organization's collective purpose with people's individual purpose – as employee, customer or wider stakeholder.

This raises the stakes such that brands now have to be deeply authentic otherwise they run the risk of alienating an increasingly discerning customer base that does not appreciate incongruence.

Evocative leaders therefore focus on inside-out branding. This is when the creative energy of the organization reaches a tipping point and wants to burst forth into the world. The challenge is to put in place branding and design frameworks that give this creative energy form, focus and utility.

With technology becoming part of every problem and every solution, we are only scratching the surface of how to build brands in digital space. Most of us in Gen X are still applying our analogue mindsets to this new digital world. It's the digital natives who will of course reshape the world of branding.

And, if design is classically about creating the material world around us, then the fourth realm invites designers into our immaterial world. This is the world of signs, symbols and artefacts.

This is the work of the artisan, of the storyteller, of the container builder. This is the art of transforming energy into form, making the invisible visible and the unconscious conscious.

This is where ritual and ceremony break free of their dogmatic religious overtones and are remembered as tools to help us through important thresholds in our lives and in our work.

Designing ritual and ceremony is about interrupting the constant monkey chatter of our mind, disempowering our egos, and thereby allowing us to surrender to more creative and co-creative frequencies. This is why leaders need to also become designers.

8. BIOLOGICAL ORGANIZING STRUCTURES

Last but not least is how stepping over this threshold opens up a wider set of organizing principles and possibilities.

Post-conventional leaders play with structure. Probably the most enlightened leader that we have ever worked with recently split his organization from a handful of business units into 20 or so cells. He intentionally made it more complex. When you dig beneath the surface of this intervention you discover that his intention was and is to force the system into working at new and novel intersections. It's not the parts that are the wellspring for future growth, it is the latent space between. This is also a clever way of forcing his senior leaders to step over the critical threshold from achiever to shaper, as he is conscious of the more subtle skills and competences that his leaders now need to develop. If he wasn't operating from the fourth realm, and was instead operating from an achiever mindset, this would have been a very dangerous move to have made, and would likely have led to dire commercial consequences.

One other example I encountered recently was at a global R&D company. The story I was told was how the global finance officer had asked the head of R&D about their innovation pipeline and what they should be expecting by when. The head of R&D replied by saying:

> 'We haven't got a clue. What we do is create the conditions that optimize our chance of success. We don't know how it works, it just does. We will get breakthroughs this year as we have done year on year for as long as we can remember. Our organization is able to swiftly adapt to what emerges and is great at taking it to market. I don't intend to mess with this magic formula.'

We need to spend more time learning about these quantum containers in the hope that when we observe them we don't collapse them.

Biological organizing structures are relatively new territory. I don't as yet have many public examples and stories to point to other than Google, WL Gore & Associates and the US Forest Service whose unorthodox organizational forms (current and historic) are common knowledge. What I do believe is the usual mechanistic matrices and silos are now holding organizations back, keeping them stuck in conventional cultural forms.

Post-conventional leaders raise their awareness, and focus their attention, on how organizations can be more like living organisms. The author, speaker and consultant, Myron E Rogers would challenge us to understand three things in this regard: How living systems work? How this living system works? How I work in and with this system?

Myron's work massively influenced another colleague of mine, John Atkinson, the former managing director of the Leadership Centre for Local Government, who pioneered the concept of Total Place.

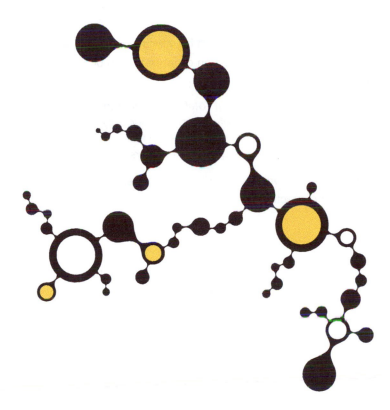

FIGURE 5.9 Biological organizing structures

This initiative looked at how a 'whole area' approach to public services would lead to better services at lower cost. It was designed to identify and avoid overlaps and duplications between organizations and to deliver step change in service improvement and efficiency at the local level, as well as across national government.

In short, Total Place looked at how local governments should shift their focus from leading an organization to understanding how to lead 'a place'.

> 'One of the central ideas of Total Place is that the longstanding machine metaphor of organization and social systems is handicapping our ability to understand the environment we work in and how to change the behaviours of those systems.'

During his work with the Leadership Centre, Myron described five major characteristics of living systems:

Chaos and complexity

Complex systems are characterized by ambiguity, uncertainty and unexpected connections. Order arises from chaotic and unmanaged micro-interactions.

Emergence

Living systems seem chaotic and unpredictable but their patterns are created by simple underlying rules that are not usually apparent to the actors.

Cognition

No one person can ever 'see the system'. Each person will have a different perspective depending on their place in the system and what they see determines what they do.

Networks

People are strongly linked by their informal ties and by the stories they tell. If the 'official line' does not fit with the lived reality of players, they will ignore or subvert it.

Self-organization

Social systems preserve their identity. Once a group or organization has formed a loyalty, people will act to hold on to the identity they have created.

I think these characteristics are great, and I can catch glimpses of how they would manifest themselves in community contexts and in local places. The challenge, of course, is how these characteristics, and others, help us to redesign and to reshape new organizing forms that are multinational, multi-locational, and multicultural – creating ecologies of innovation and resource.

There is no one right answer. I really hope we see a plethora of experimental organizational forms in the next few years, designed to leverage diversity, focus on connection and intersection, hold creative tension and enable their people to ride both the highs and lows of the creative process.

This is a massively exciting space to explore.

SUMMARY

These eight value-adding and capturing capacities are particularly prominent in my world. I'm sure I've missed many other things that become available to businesses and governments alike when they step over this subtle threshold.

My hope is that I've outlined them enough to help you feel into them and to illuminate some of the new value-creating opportunities that exist in and from the fourth realm. Moreover, companies that are experimenting with stepping over this subtle threshold, whether they know they are doing it or not, are the ones, from where I stand, that are the innovators and shapers of our time.

What I'd like to do in the next few chapters is to go into more detail about:

- what it means to create containers and hold spaces for riding the creative rollercoaster;

- what states and qualities of mind help us ride the creative rollercoaster (and what states of mind increase our likelihood of flatlining);

- what it means to tune organizational cultures to the music of innovation; and

- ultimately, summarize the subtle skills of post-conventional leadership.

THICKENING SPACE

In 1993, as a postgraduate at a London design school, I co-founded a community called the Design Transformation Group (DTG) – a not-for-profit learning community of designers, artists, educationalists, philosophers, consultants and futurologists, who were all passionate about shaping the future business of design.

It came into being as we networked into the mavericks and the pioneers, noticing that by definition, and not intent, they lacked any sense of community. What would a community of individualists look like? This was a creative dilemma too sexy not to explore, so we designed and ran two biennial, one-week-long, DesignQuests, where this community of between 40 and 60 people came together from around the world to just play with possibilities. Every other year we then published a book based on what had happened.

It was mad. These people were out there, and my particular role was to hold the community in co-creative process. This was a 'jump-in-the-deep-end-and-learn-how-to-swim' experience for me.

The first thing I learned was that co-creative communities leverage diversity. Sparks began to fly at the creative intersections of different skills, talents and gifts. It was mind-blowing to watch. One minute there was a group looking at 'language and the mind', and another looking at 'individualism and possession'. Then we would dive into the mystery of 'phenomenology' and then 'the nature of interconnectedness'. The diversity of topics that we traversed was incredible. More interesting still were the creative notions that emerged in the space between.

As with any community it also had to evolve through various stages of development. I remember on the second day of the second DesignQuest, held in a hexagonal fort on the Isle of Wight off the south coast of England, that one of the participants kept monologueing in the community sessions. He was unconsciously (if I was being generous) trying to be the centre of attention, to the extent that his behaviour was distracting the wider community. Everyone could feel the energy of the event leaking and not building in momentum. The challenge was how to intervene without shaming and ultimately alienating him.

At the 'open space' sessions at the end of the day I spoke to the community about behaviours that would optimize the co-creative space between us all and behaviours that would undermine our collective potential. I used myself as an example, disclosing what I believed to be some of my own distorted behaviours when I'm out of my comfort zone. As soon as I disclosed my own vulnerabilities so did others. And so did our temporary culprit. As soon as he did (and to be fair, with a good amount of self-awareness) you could feel the energy of the community move to a whole other level.

I learned subsequently that compassionately speaking your truth, in real time, thickens the space between us, creating the fertile ground from which the new can emerge.

FIGURE 6.1 DTG community

06

CREATING CONTAINERS AND HOLDING SPACES

Riding the creative rollercoaster starts with a burning question. Not a statement wrapped up as a question, but a question we really don't know the answer to. It needs to be a question that if we could break through it, we would significantly leap forward.

Shaping a great question is more difficult than it sounds. We could brainstorm a series of ideas and get really excited about them, and then tomorrow we'd wake up, review them and think, 'What a load of crap'.

A breakthrough question (a question that lights a creative fire in us) needs to resonate with us in such a way that it will hold our attention over a sustained period of time. It needs to point us squarely into the unknown and challenge us in every moment of every day, until we have had the breakthrough.

It is also not a static thing as it will often morph and refine over time as our assumptions and ingrained beliefs start to drop away.

For this to happen we need to hold the question rather than answer the question. If we try to answer it directly we diminish its power. For as soon as we answer a question, we stop being curious, we stop learning, and most certainly the next iteration of the breakthrough question won't show itself. Instead, we get trapped within our existing paradigm.

By holding the breakthrough question lightly in front of us, with clear intent, it begins to open a space within us, a pregnant void, ready for the new to show itself.

If leaders and teams are to transcend their already honed delivery skills, and start to develop their discovery skills, then shaping and sculpting the most important questions that they and their organization need to break through is a fantastic starting point. Breakthrough questions play a critical role in catalysing the music of innovation. And, an ecology of breakthrough questions lies at the heart of a great strategy.

Placing the right questions into an organization can be more powerful that putting the right answers into it, for they interrupt an important cultural trap, the fear of making mistakes. You cannot answer a breakthrough question without making lots of mistakes. They facilitate an iterative process of trial and error (and I love the fact that the root of the word error means to wander). You have to plan for failure at the front end of the process. If you don't fail then you don't leap forward.

I look forward to the day when it is okay to have a meeting that fails, because we understand that we are in the low, the dip, of the creative process. Without this being okay we collapse the tension and jump to a premature conclusion and likely to a remedial action.

With temporary failure being okay, our next challenge is to maintain the creative tension and emotional frustration, and use it as fuel to power us into the unknown.

Once you have got the right question (or questions), the next part of creating the container is bringing the right people together, for the right time, in the right place, with the right

FIGURE 6.2 Breakthrough questions

design (human process). This sounds simple but even these foundational elements of container-building are just not the norm in most organizations. Riding the creative rollercoaster is not a one-hour meeting slotted into our Outlook diary.

Don't pass go until you have worked out the right people to be in the room and on the journey. Fudge this and the game is over. Put the effort into creating a sense of rightness, because the team itself will unconsciously know if the right people are involved or not. Have one or two interlopers and they will be, because of no fault of their own, energetic drains on the group, at a time when the container needs to be watertight.

Seek diversity of thought, even contradiction of opinion. Pay attention to who cares most, and who will have to implement post-breakthrough. Don't be seduced by hierarchy. Instead mix wisdom with naivety. And every so often throw in a cynic.

Cynics are at one level a pain in the ass. At another they represent an important part of the equation, for they represent aspects of our shadow selves. Holding a cynic through this type of journey takes an enormous amount of energy. Yet, cynics can switch, often becoming the greatest advocates.

To this day I try to include a vocal cynic when we are doing deep transformation work. At the top of global corporations, there is no shortage of them. And, when they switch they can become the epicentres of transformational change.

Next we come to the right time and place. As I've mentioned before, creative meetings are not like operational meetings. Sitting around a table with loads of PowerPoint presentations, in a room with no windows, is hardly conducive to co-creating new meaning, new thoughts and new solutions. Yet this is the way most meetings are held, give or take a few windows.

A creative or co-creative meeting requires a different type of preparation. It has a different rhythm. And it has a different shape – metaphorically, energetically and literally.

You can ride a mini creative rollercoaster in three hours – 90 minutes if you have collectively developed the skill.

It usually takes the form of lots of short inputs around a breakthrough question, followed by a creative dialogue where the group moves through the phases of politeness, conflict, enquiry and finally glimpses of generative flow.

Some creative rollercoasters take two to three days to ride, and benefit enormously from being off-site and residential. Using evenings to leverage the hypnagogic and hypnopompic states, just before we fall to sleep and just after we wake from sleep, enables teams to tap into other ways of knowing. It is amazing how much more productive a one-day meeting is when it starts the evening before.

Some creative rollercoasters can take weeks, months, and occasionally years to ride. In this instance they are formed from sequences and layers of meetings, workshops, gatherings and empty spaces.

Whatever their length and level of intensity, riding a creative rollercoaster requires quality time and space. Unfortunately, the habit of senior leaders is to want to bolt these types of 'odd' meetings on to existing meetings. Or they want to reduce a three-hour creative session to an hour. This doesn't work!

The irony is, investing three days to ride the highs and lows of the creative process will save at the very least three months of circular conversations and the inevitable loss of energy and time. This is without mentioning the leakage of value from the sub-optimal solutions that result from doing what you've always done.

When teams learn about what it takes to ride the creative rollercoaster they stop being victims of time, and start learning how to speed up and slow down time. These teams learn to mix it up, where in the morning a leadership team might sit around their boardroom table, running through a list of operational priorities and updates; and in the afternoon move to a different room, sit in a circle, slow down and deep-dive into a few strategic and creative questions. The former is dominated by inputs and a minimal amount of 'exchange' – discussion, questions for clarification, feedback and decision making. The latter is more dynamic, with shorter inputs at the front end to contextualize and bring to life the breakthrough question, followed by the team, group or community awakening and tapping into their collective intelligence.

While an operational meeting is agenda-based, a creative or even strategic meeting is design-based. What I mean by this is a designed sequence of human processes that enable the team to ride the different phases and stages of the creative rollercoaster. This first stage we call: 'It's all in the prep'.

Shaping the right question(s), freeing up the right people, for the right amount of time, with the right space and design is the work. The chances of success and breakthrough is maximized in the preparation stage. Get this wrong, or underestimate the importance of preparation, and you suffer the consequences.

A quick aside. We design and catalyse a lot of co-creative conferences, the front end of which is usually the opportunity for the hosting leadership team to step forward, outline the context and set the challenge.

Now in the design and preparation stage our intent is to interrupt orthodoxy, which nine out of ten times is death by PowerPoint, with each input being on average an hour long.

Our challenge back to the leadership team is to deliver all inputs during the first half-day, freeing up the remaining time to work co-creatively with the assembled community. This means most inputs need to be between 10 and 20 minutes long.

Designing and delivering a 10-minute talk is a lot harder than rambling through a 60-minute presentation. Often leaders deliver key messages better in a shorter time frame. But here's

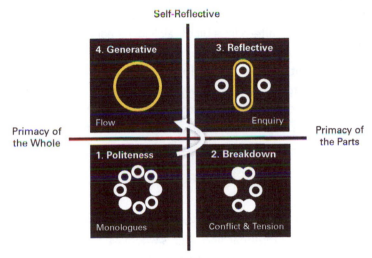

FIGURE 6.3 Creative dialogue
Based on the work of Bill Isaacs

the rub. Most leaders are not used to formally rehearsing their conference inputs. So we insist that the day before a conference begins, that they set aside time for a full rehearsal of all key inputs. And moreover, all speakers need to see and give feedback to one other.

The resistance to this simple request is usually, 'We don't need to rehearse'. This is code for, 'I am too senior and important to rehearse'. So, after a little bit of cajoling, rehearsal time arrives. And, every time we do this, their presentations become at least 300 per cent more potent. Moreover, they join up their key messages into a coherent, flowing whole. The container is now set for us to do co-creative work together in real time, whether there are 60 people in the room or 600. It's all in the prep!

ON-BOARDING

It's all in the prep is the first stage creative rollercoaster (as Map). We call it On-Boarding. This is where we slow everything down. This can be excruciatingly painful for those people that are 'doers' in the room, who just want to get on. Just getting on means doing the same as before. This is the time to on-board the group or team to the breakthrough question(s), to the strategic context, to the challenge, to the need/imperative (to the what and the whys); as well as to each other and to new ways of working.

This is the time to slow down (Stage 2) and remember what we (individually and collectively) already know. We call this mapping the island of knowledge. This often includes everyone in

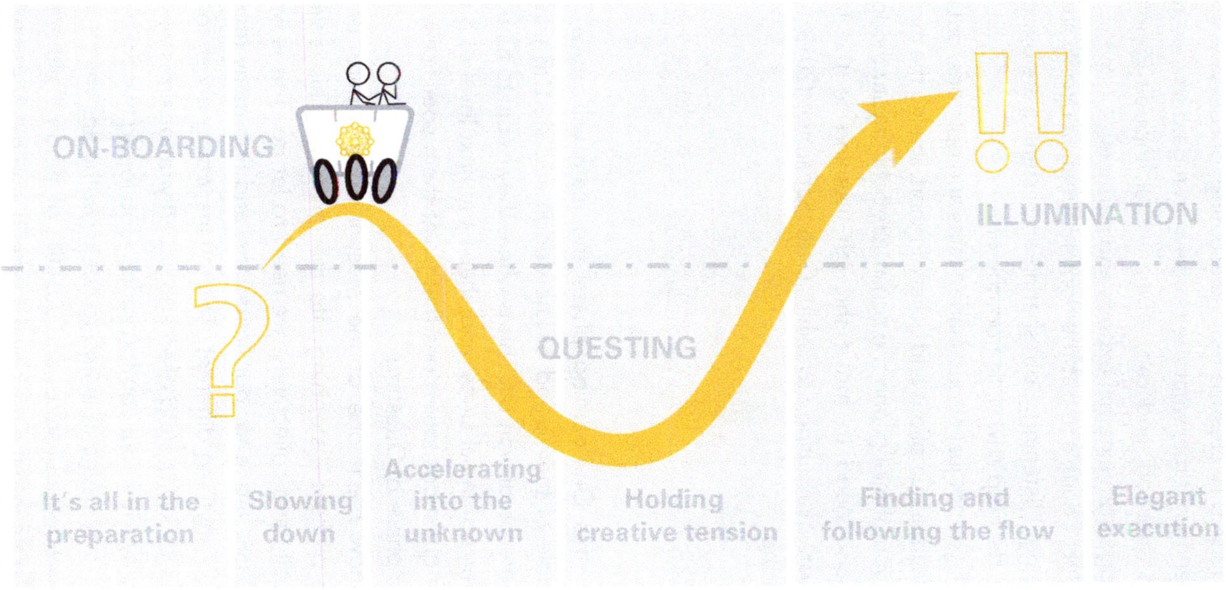
ON-BOARDING
QUESTING
ILLUMINATION
It's all in the preparation
Slowing down
Accelerating into the unknown
Holding creative tension
Finding and following the flow
Elegant execution

FIGURE 6.4 Phases and stages of the creative rollercoaster

the leadership or creative team presenting (of course in a very short period of time) what they know with regard to the breakthrough question, and can, where useful, include importing knowledge from external experts and partners.

The focus here is to get the right information openly shared with the right listening. Both sharing and listening are opportunities to develop new skills from the off.

Sharing is not just about sharing facts and opinions, but also hopes, fears, assumptions and beliefs. In short, sharing the thinking behind your thinking, and the constructs behind your thoughts.

We also need to move through listening to the facts, to empathic listening, to what Otto Scharmer (2013) calls 'presencing'.

QUESTING

Even in this On-Boarding phase the team will move from the middle of their island of knowledge and start to explore their shoreline of wonder. This is where they begin to tune into an ecology of initial clues, and shape the next level of breakthrough questions, questions that point them specifically into the next phase of Questing.

We now reach one of the most important parts of the creative process – stepping into the unknown. This is when, individually and collectively, we need to let go. This is where we so easily argue for our limitations, and find many reasons not to do anything different. This means letting go of control while our tricksy bastard of an ego expertly rationalizes why we should stay within our comfort zones. God forbid that we might be seen to be vulnerable and to not know the answer.

This is where our states and qualities of mind will either help us accelerate into the unknown (Stage 3), and help us truly ride

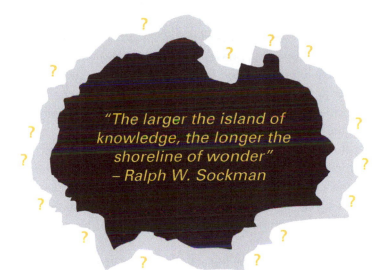

FIGURE 6.5 Island of knowledge, shoreline of wonder

the highs and lows of the creative rollercoaster; or they will collapse the process and bring us all back to flatlining. I will outline these states and qualities more fully in the next chapter.

Let's assume for the moment, that we now tip into the next phase of Questing. This means getting lost, staying with the creative tension (Stage 4) and finding and following the flow (Stage 5) of the clues and questions that have the greatest energy and resonance. This means moving from a rational choice to an energetic one.

Often when we have lots of marks spread on the floor from the initial On-Boarding phase, we can feel overwhelmed by not being able to see the wood for the trees. But if you stay with it, and tune into other ways of knowing, then the most energetic and field-charged clues start to reveal themselves. They emerge from the background into the foreground.

Let me try to make this more real. Back in the Nineties my doctoral research was on how to catalyse moments of optimal experience, and I grabbed the opportunity to teach drawing to both first-year (novice) and third-year (expert) art students.

I learned a number of important lessons that have stayed with me ever since.

First, I was touched by the act of 'drawing' itself. My mentor and PhD supervisor at the time, Dr Geoffrey Bailey, wrote:

> 'A drawing is the result of draw-ing. A drawing directly reflects the drawer's creative experience of bringing the drawing into existence. It is never a solution. It is always an opportunity.
>
> A drawing presents us with a way of personalizing and interpreting the world through the application of marks on a surface. Yet, drawing is not simply the rehearsal of graphic mark-making, but the seeking of meaningful connections formed through new seeing and ordering.
>
> Aspects of the drawing may be recognizable, bring forward dormant memories, or construct new thought,

but drawing is primarily an activity of discovery arising from a processing of subjective expression and physical gesture, creating a direct relationship between the image made and the act of making it.'

What I learned from this is that innovation is born of creativity, and creativity is born of making marks in the world. Without mark-making (physically and metaphorically) we fall into trying to create in a vacuum. Rather, creativity is the awareness that emerges out of the creative tension between possibilities and limitations.

Second, if we make enough marks, new patterns emerge in the space between. This is fundamentally different to the notion within brainstorming where volume is king, and that from the many you will find a few good ideas. Let me bring this to life more fully with another drawing example. When you ask most novice drawers to draw a figure on a sheet of paper, using pencil or charcoal, the usual sequence they follow is to start with the head, move down to the shoulders and arms, torso, legs and then feet. The only problem is that by the time they get to the feet there's no more room. The figure doesn't fit on the page. They've miscalculated the position and scale of the figure such that the feet fall off the page. This is a typical linear approach – from head to toe.

The more experienced drawer would start by marking small marks all over the page, feeling into the space and the possibility. They would layer mark upon mark, building a background that in time allows the foreground – the figure itself – to emerge. This is an emergent approach that allows new order to emerge from chaos and new pattern to emerge from complexity.

With this core skill we can now start to play with new and novel intersections in the space between one another, between our assumptions, our beliefs, our lived experiences and our emerging matrix of clues.

During this Questing phase we follow the clues and start to experience mini-insights (fleeting moments where meaning is reordered), which again we map. In mapping them we can continue to feel the whole and are able to lean into the emerging future, as opposed to insights getting lost in the ether or lost in translation.

The Questing phase is not about making meaning of the new insights. Rather it is about learning to traverse and live in the unknown. All we need to do is find and follow the flow. Map an insight and let that insight point you to your next quest, to find the next clue and the next insight, and so on and so forth. Follow what has energy. Park what doesn't. Resist the temptation to find the answer. Sink into the unknown. Relish not knowing. This is where the creative tension builds and we need to hold it, not collapse it. And, this is where exponential learning takes place, as our assumptions start to drop away and our beliefs become more fluid.

We now start to think, relate, learn and organize things differently. We start catching glimpses of an intelligence wider than our own. Every intersection, and in turn, every space between becomes full of possibility. What was invisible becomes visible. What was unconscious becomes conscious. What was implicate becomes explicate.

This capacity to stay with the creative tension, to stay with the pain, is another one of the magic ingredients of riding the creative rollercoaster. I've therefore come to believe that pain is a critical part of change. I see so many leaders over-protect their people, and thereby remove or dilute the emotional components of moving through new thresholds of personal and professional development. Of course I'm not advocating pain for pain's sake. Nor am I advocating any ounce of pleasure in putting people through pain. I do believe, though, that we need to see pain as a part of growth. Holding spaces that allow people to work through their pain (particularly the pain of letting go of what they know, or what they think they know) is a great skill most leaders misunderstand.

Moreover, as any struggling artist or writer will tell you, the creative process itself is all about riding the highs and the lows. These highs and lows are emotional as much as they are physical, conceptual or intellectual. Learning to ride the highs and lows of the creative process is one of the central tenets of catalysing creative insight and collective breakthrough. The lows generate the creative energy needed to reach new highs. By embracing and intentionally designing in the lows, you can learn to reach the highs more often and for longer periods of time.

ILLUMINATION

Lastly we come to the phase of *Illumination*. Ideally there is some down-time before this phase. This allows our unconscious to incubate the emerging patterns. This could be over an evening, or could be over weeks or months.

This is a natural phenomenon. When your mind is given a question it cannot answer your unconscious processes go into overdrive. It hates incomplete Gestalts. This is what we take advantage of individually and collectively, when we want to tap into the collective unconscious of a group.

What then happens is our unconscious mind starts to crack the code. The problem is, our unconscious mind doesn't speak to us in everyday language as our conscious thoughts do. Instead, our unconscious mind works with symbol, pattern, synchronicity, serendipity, repetition and energy. As we become more present and more attuned, we start to catch glimpses of the clues that our unconscious mind is pointing us towards. The trick is to get our everyday consciousness out of the way.

Our unconscious answers breakthrough questions much, much faster than our everyday mind. The challenge is to listen and lean into what life is teaching us, ie what our unconscious mind is pointing us towards. Again, this is both an individual and a collective phenomenon.

Then it is rather like the previous drawing example. Suddenly the picture starts to reveal itself. It literally breaks through the surface of our existing worldview and re-patterns it in a moment of illumination. What emerges can sometimes be a 'wow' moment. More often than not it is an 'of course' moment, where the new reveals itself simultaneously with hindsight.

What emerges are innovative outputs, which are other than us, objective, independent and distinguished; as well as transformational outcomes, ie we have changed through the process. How we see and make meaning of the world has been challenged and reordered. We can't go backwards, only forwards.

We can now move into verification, implementation and execution, through rapid prototyping, optimizing performance and scaling success. This is why the creative rollercoaster can also massively aid productivity, not just creativity and innovation.

A lot of projects are perceived to fail because of poor execution. This is sometimes true. It is also true that a lot of projects are set up to fail. The desire and habit to get on, to move to premature action, to take short-cuts in resourcing and to push things through to resolution before they are sufficiently cooked, are just as much to blame.

If leaders and teams could learn to slow down at the front end, get the scope, focus and resource in place with beauty and skill, then there would be less busy-ness (our way of masking our inadequacies) and more productive workplaces. This in turn would free up more time and space to step into and inhabit the fourth realm of the innovator/shaper.

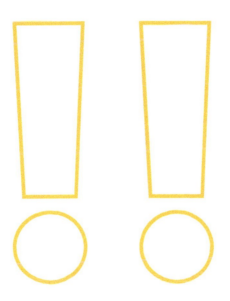

FIGURE 6.6 Double exclamation marks

SUMMARY

The creative rollercoaster is a map for creating containers and holding spaces that accelerate us towards moments of creative insight and breakthrough, and where the old adage 'slow down to go fast' literally plays out.

There are three main phases:

- On-Boarding;

- Questing;

- and Illumination.

And, there are six main stages:

- It's all in the preparation!

- Slowing down;

- Accelerating into the unknown;

- Holding creative tension;

- Finding and following the flow; and

- Elegant execution.

Mastering these phases and stages is a lifelong journey as we discover ever-decreasing circles, ie there's always a better way. We have also learned that creating containers and holding spaces begins from within.

BREAKDOWN BEFORE BREAKTHROUGH

As I've already mentioned, being in hospital as a teenager was life-changing. For a few years thereafter I actively felt the need to seek the meaning of life. Some teenagers do this through the lyrics of songs, but I can never remember lyrics. In fact I have never learned to hear lyrics. For some reason they don't register in my brain at all. Instead, I explored different religions and spiritual traditions, as well as jumped into many life-affirming books. For example, I was extremely inspired by the book *Jonathan Livingston Seagull*, and others in the series. I explored Taoism, Sufism and Christianity. I also tried engaging with great thinkers, from the philosopher Nietzsche, to the anthropologist and cyberneticist Gregory Bateson. Ultimately I was drawn to Zen Buddhism. I loved the discipline of it. I loved the creative stillness it evoked. I loved the fact that it was 'a way of life' rather than a belief in a god-like deity.

I was mesmerized by how its disciplines were designed to liberate our consciousness.

While I initially studied the Japanese Soto school of Zen with its focus on *zazen* (quiet and mindful meditation leading to gradual openings), in time I became more drawn to studying the Rinzai school of Zen and its use of *kõans* (seemingly paradoxical conundrums and questions upon which we meditate, that are designed to lead to sudden openings).

In a professional sense, I found *kōans* to be an amazing and mystical pedagogic technique, at a time when I was interested in experiencing and gathering a portfolio of creative tools and techniques.

Zen also introduced me to the notion of liberating-disciplines – disciplines that use designed constraints to liberate us from our own limitations. *Kōan* study taught me that breakthrough is always preceded by some kind of breakdown of core constructs (ego, context, assumptions, beliefs), manifesting as creative tension. The trouble in today's world is that we have forgotten how to hold ourselves in creative tension. More often than not we collapse back to our points of positional difference, back into politeness and back into our comfort zones.

Building upon the power of disbelief – 'I didn't know I could do that?' – I therefore became interested not in spiritual enlightenment but in creative enlightenment, how to catalyse moments of creative insight whereby our sense of self expands as we literally break through into a new reality. And more importantly, where breakthrough happens by design.

STATES AND QUALITIES OF MIND

'Innovation flourishes at the intersection of diverse experience, whether it be others' or our own.'

– The Innovator's DNA

For well over a decade now we have been developing a new model of leadership designed to help executive and senior leaders step into and lead from the fourth realm. This model sees resource as energy. It outlines the cornerstones of cultures of innovation. It describes the characteristics of creative teams. It challenges leaders to evoke the music of innovation; and, it points to how they can develop their voltage (their ability to work with and hold the potential difference between the highs and lows of the creative process) and their capacity (their ability to be bigger than the greatest disturbance in the room or system).

It also builds upon the premise that creating containers and holding spaces starts from within. Is there the internal space for the new to arise? Can we hold diversity in creative juxtaposition? Do we know how to work with tension, other than retain it as emotional or physical stress?

This model of leadership identifies *four states of mind* and *four qualities of mind*. Together they form an Evocative Leadership Circle, designed to help ourselves, our teams and our organizations step into the fourth realm and ride the creative rollercoaster.

THE FOUR STATES OF MIND

The first state of mind is *creative fire*. Do we have a burning passion? Are we driven by a compelling purpose? What are our sources of inspiration? This fire can be very palpable. You can often feel its heat.

Evocative leaders build and stoke this fire because they understand how it acts as an energetic wellspring, challenging and exciting teams and organizations to ask the big questions and to break free of their limitations. This state and trait has a bursting forth energy, radiating new possibilities at every turn to shape, make and co-create the future.

In contrast to this, evocative leaders also pay attention to the health of their systems. While creative fire burns energy and resources at a pace, evocative leaders know how important it is to replenish this energy and nurture their teams and organizations.

They therefore invest in and understand the importance of developing the *wholeness* of their organization – its intellectual, social, emotional, physical and spiritual capital – so as to refuel its creativity. They often secure this state of mind by designing structures and organizing mechanisms that support growth and foster longevity.

The third state of mind that evocative leaders pay attention to is their team's and/or their organization's capacity to work with and venture into the *unknown*. This means increasing levels of curiosity, deepening the quality of relationships, developing

FIGURE 7.1 Four states of mind

emotional intelligence and resilience, and expanding trust. These qualities resource teams and organizations to step into the unknown, to work with uncertainty and to muster the resolve needed to continuously walk through the world with a sense of awe and wonder.

The final state of mind is *elegant action.* This is the capacity to move like a flock of birds. This is about 'drawing beautiful lines in the world'. It is not a workman-like energy. Rather, this state is all about finding and following the flow of creative expression ie turning purposeful energy into innovative form.

To catalyse this phenomenon evocative leaders deploy sets of liberating-disciplines designed to focus the creative energy of their teams and their organizations, helping them move into optimal states of flow.

THE BOW AND ARROW

These four states of individual and collective mind also hold a deeper code for creating post-conventional containers. The East-West axis of this Evocative Leadership Circle is called 'the Bow', as it is about putting creative (ie constructive) tension into human systems.

The Bow recognizes that we first need to stand in our 'differences' before we can work with our 'wholeness'. When the going gets tough, as it inevitably will when riding the creative rollercoaster, we need to be strong in our unique sense of self, what sets us apart, and what lights our fire. Then, and only then, are we able to come into creative relationships with others.

Lose our sense of self and difference and we collapse the creative potential of new and novel intersections. We are then unable to lean into the empty spaces that emerge between the crisscrosses of intersections.

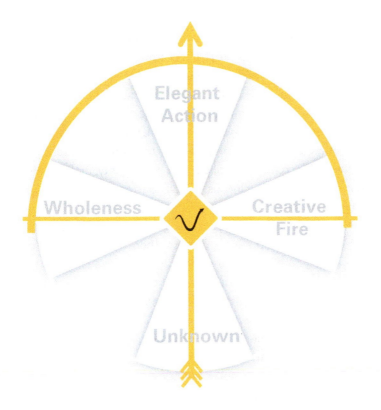

FIGURE 7.2 The bow and arrow

The challenge is to simultaneously hold a sense of part and whole. This is a prerequisite before stepping into the unknown, otherwise fear will manifest from within, and in the space between, making us wobble, collapse the creative tension and reduce our individual and shared experiences to a flat line.

Next comes 'the Arrow'. This South-North axis is about finding and following flow. This starts with our ability to let go, to surrender our egos, to be still and completely open. There is often a direct correlation with our level of trust in ourselves and in those around us. This trust is born of the quality of relationship and the level of emotional intelligence we can generate with others. Without this stability and resilience, formed in the core of a creative container, we start to overreact emotionally to the growing tension (filled with uncertainty, unfamiliarity, lack of control...), forcing us to hold on too tightly to what is familiar and safe.

However, if we invest in building containers that can hold our differences and our wholeness, then the feathers of our arrow are more likely to fly straight and true. We can then pull the arrow back into the unknown, further increase the tension and continue to hold a state of openness and readiness, waiting for the right moment to arise.

Letting that moment come, by leaning into it, then becomes like a hunter preparing to pounce on its prey. Our quality of attention and intent determines our capacity to move at the right time and through space with speed and elegance – so we hit our target square on.

The critical difference to this hunting analogy is that we don't know what the target is in the creative process. It arises in the moment, and we need to grab it in a moment. These moments are fleeting and fragile. It is important to learn to see them and respect them as such.

Judge them too soon and too harshly and they just float away. Unconditionally tend and attend to them, and they might actually show us something new.

Get these things right, and when we let the arrow go it pulls that which was previously unseen into the light, bringing the new to mind, and bringing the new to the world.

THE FOUR QUALITIES OF MIND

While the *four states of mind* determine our *voltage*, the *four qualities of mind* determine our *capacity*. They also enable and amplify the four states of mind.

I've already mentioned the first quality of mind – *presencing*. For me, presencing is the ability to live and work in the here and now, to be still, to appreciate the gift of the present, to perceive beauty in the detail, to attend to what is needed or missing, to awaken all of our senses, to feel into our uniqueness, and to love life.

Within the context of evocative leadership, presencing gives us the creative stillness needed to catch the sparks of the new as they emerge from the creative fire. Presencing also resources leaders to walk the fine line between power and danger more mindfully. This is part and parcel of stepping into the unknown. With presence we can stay balanced and retain our emotional resilience in the face of uncertainty and fear.

The second quality of mind is *patterning*. This skill enables us to find pattern in complexity, order in chaos, and to allow innovative foregrounds to emerge from strategic backgrounds. It resources us to see and feel into the future by tuning into the natural cycles and rhythms of life; to work with timing and ripeness, to understand creative interdependencies, and to play with new and novel connections

This subtle skill helps us tap into our wholeness. It also helps us tune into creative rhythms, enabling us to act, or strike, with the power, precision and timing of a martial artist.

The third quality of mind is *story-ing*. By this I don't mean being a good orator. Instead, I mean using the power of intention to subtly affect the future – to story it into reality. Some leaders have this uncanny ability to tell stories about what they intend to make and shape, and in their speaking of it they make it more likely to happen. It's as if the universe bends to them and them to it.

This subtle skill aligns where we have come from, with where we are, with our intention for the future. It also opens up space for others to enfold themselves into a bigger story, attuning individual and collective purpose while also creating a deep sense of belonging. This allows everyone to find his or her rightful place of strength and contribution.

This sense of direction is a critical resource when we step into the unknown. It also challenges us to ensure we are fit (healthy and whole) for purpose.

The fourth quality of mind is *de-signing*. This is the ability to transform energy into form so as to make and shape new meaning in the world. To do this leaders need to become the catalyst for change. They need to keep their energy clear and bright, listen and to all voices and perspectives. For, when the new emerges from a deep source of integrity, it vibrates in such a way as to exude vital energy, ie it becomes a strange attractor.

FIGURE 7.3 Four qualities of mind

This last quality and skill helps us use our energy efficiently as it enables us to execute actions with elegance and grace. It also enables us to fan the flames of creative fire.

Finally, these four qualities of mind work in pairs. Presencing and patterning are all about *bringing the new to mind*; while story-ing and de-signing are all about *bringing the new to the world.* Together they allow us to lean into the emerging future, find and follow flow and catalyse creative insight and collective breakthrough.

DISTORTIONS

Unfortunately there are two things that can easily get in the way of riding the creative rollercoaster: 'me' and 'us'.

We all have ingrained habits in the way we walk through the world. They also influence the way we think and the way we relate to others.

These habits distort our reality and our relationships, taking us out of co-creative relationship with the world and with friends, family and colleagues. Let me share the wheel of distortions.

Superior mind

This distortion triggers us to feel superior, thinking we are better than others. We start to look down on other people, quick to dismiss their ideas, contributions and opinions. This separates us from our creative fire, takes us out of creative relationship with significant others, and presents us as aloof, distant and arrogant.

Indulgent mind

This distortion triggers us to overindulge and fall into addictive behaviours that might include gossiping, shopping, drinking,

FIGURE 7.4 Wheel of distortions

eating and other more health-threatening habits. These defence mechanisms mask our feelings of emptiness or numbness, leading to an inability to stay present and connected from moment to moment.

Circus mind

This distortion triggers emotional overreactions to the ups and downs of life. It seeks out and feeds on drama and trauma – positive or negative. This knocks us off balance, leading to knee-jerk rather than mindful responses. It also generates fear and doubt, causing us to close down more productive, life-affirming options.

Maya mind

This distortion triggers unhelpful delusions or illusions that distract us and take us off track. We get lost in the maze of life. We lose our sense of purpose and direction, and instead float through life like a leaf in the wind. We drift naively from one thing to the next, standing for nothing, and falling for anything.

Victim mind

This distortion triggers a victim mentality, a feeling of being done to, and feeling powerless to do anything about it. It's like we have no choice, leading to feelings of burden, resentment, anger and worthlessness. Ironically this leads to even more over-giving, at the cost of our own health and well-being.

Ramrod mind

This distortion triggers an out-of-balance relationship with time. We feel a tremendous pressure to prematurely push things to resolution. This encourages us to run over the top of anything and anyone in order to get things done. Behind this compulsion is an inability to trust others to deliver.

Workhorse mind

This distortion triggers an over-identification with work. At one level this results in us working all hours. At another level our sense of who we are is reduced to 'a role', such that we bring less and less of ourselves to work, and ultimately less and less of ourselves to life. We keep taking on more and more work to keep busy and feel needed.

Judgement mind

This distortion triggers overly harsh and critical judgements about self and others. We begin to see the world in terms of good and bad, right and wrong, such that we become fanatical about our views. Underlying this distortion is a need to control, closing down our ability to hear different perspectives and be open to change.

Distortions often hunt in packs, creating distorted patterns of behaviour, thought and action. Our challenge is to use the four states and four qualities of consciousness to interrupt them.

THE DIAMOND

The more embodied these four states and four qualities of mind are, the more potent the space a leader can hold.

Evocative leaders use their bodies as a tool for holding *space*. This is how leadership comes through us, literally. They become shape-shifters. They learn how to play with their length, width and depth so as either to intentionally take up space or intentionally reduce their space ie when to be visible and when to be invisible. They also learn how to extend their creative energy into the world in non-linear ways that charge and prime the field for change.

Evocative leaders also play with *time*. While the physics of time is constant, and biological time is regular, psychological time can be sped up and slowed down. Time is different in character to space as time flows in one direction – forward – and is always causal. For example, the creative rollercoaster only ever goes forward. When it goes up, it then must come down.

Holding co-creative spaces requires leaders to intentionally speed up and slow down psychological time.

The American psychologist Abraham Maslow (1968) famously described time in relation to peak love experiences where:

> 'Time passes in their ecstasies such that a day may flash by as if it were a minute, and that a minute may be so passionately lived that it feels like a day.'

Meanwhile, the Hungarian psychologist Mihaly Csikszentmihalyi (1990) describes how the letting go of judgement and reason opens the doors to optimal states of flow, which in turn lead us into deeper levels of subjective awareness. I'm sure this disorientation, or elasticity, of subjective time and space as a phenomenon will be familiar to us all.

So playing with time is a critical ingredient in designing and catalysing creative rollercoasters – knowing when to slow people down, and when to speed them up. Pushing, pushing, pushing at a full on, constant pace, just keeps us in our heads and overly relying on our shorter dendrites. We then have no time to incubate and no time to access more indirect pathways, associations, intersections and empty spaces.

However, let's not forget that time and space are intimately interconnected. You can speed up and slow down time just by reshaping space.

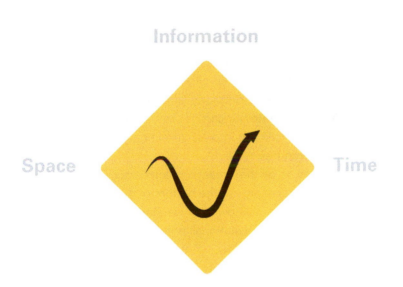

FIGURE 7.5 The diamond

Time and space are two points of the diamond that lies at the heart of the Evocative Leadership Circle. The other two points are *energy* and *information*.

Interestingly, the common definition of energy is the capacity of a system to perform work. Energy is necessary for things to change, and all living things require available energy to stay alive. Classical mechanics distinguish between potential energy of an object (a function of its position in space) and kinetic energy (a function of its movement through space-time).

The beauty of energy is that it transforms; for example, from potential chemical energy (in oil and gas) into thermal energy (generating heat and pressure) and then into mechanical energy (that accelerate our cars); or how a solar cell transforms radiant energy of the sun into electrical energy that can power a light or a computer.

In the context of the creative rollercoaster, we reach our maximum (kinetic) energy at the bottom of the curve, ironically while we are in the unknown. As we start to rise our energy gets converted into (gravitational) potential energy, as we now have new possibilities in tow.

Paying attention to the energy of a team or group is therefore vital. When it is low, don't assume you need to enliven it, as some facilitators tend to do with energizer exercises. More often than not, the need will be to stay with the tension and continue to ride the creative rollercoaster even further down into the dip.

At the other end of the spectrum, when the energy is high, know that this will be fleeting, as this is when we will be expending the most energy. Remember to relish these moments.

The challenge, therefore, is to use time, space and energy to help us more frequently experience the highs, and when we have them, to extend them for longer periods of time.

Finally we come to *information*. I remember having an argument with a very good friend of mine, and work colleague, on a beach in Malibu, while on a quest for one of our clients. Our heated debate was about what was more primary – energy or information? We didn't shy away from holding our different views. Ironically, this argument led a few weeks later to the actual breakthrough we needed. My understanding is that there is still an ongoing argument about this between physicists. But, let's not go there now.

As we ride the creative rollercoaster, we need to work with different forms of information. It is likely that we will start with conventional, fact-based, opinion-based, experience-based information. This information takes the form of the familiar signs and signal-sign systems of language.

We then need to work with clues, or information on the edges of what we know; and then with insight – delicate information that has resonance (ie radiates energy) and that gives us glimpses of the new. If we try to layer our existing paradigm over these fragile fragments of symbolic information, they simply dissolve away.

Then we need to work with pattern and sequence, at intersection, and in the space between. This is where meaning reorders, and we have to literally rede-sign ourselves in order to bring the new to mind.

Finally we need to language the new into the world as innovation.

These four primary elements – *time*, *space*, *energy* and *information* – point to the high art of riding the creative rollercoaster, the dance between the explicate (that which has already been unfolded, fragmented and distinguished) and the implicate world (that which is still enfolded, interdependent and undistinguished). Only for a few moments in my career has the everyday world dropped away such that I was co-creating with the purity of these four elements.

QUANTUM COLLAPSE

Before I wrap this chapter up, let me take one final step. One of the most interesting theories of consciousness and creativity that I came across in my doctoral research was by physicist Sir Roger Penrose (1994) and the anaesthetist and consciousness researcher Stuart Hameroff (1994). They developed a theory of the brain as a quantum mechanical process, and therefore consciousness as a quantum mechanical state.

The main principles of quantum mechanics are that sub-atomic particles are actually waves of vibratory possibilities, existing in two or more super-positional states at the same time. While in superposition these particles have their own space/time geometry. And yet, when these quantum states interact they become intimately interconnected in phase across time and space.

Quantum theory has led to the development of quantum computers that can sustain multiple and simultaneous computations, according to linear super-positions, and which finally collapse at a particular result – a self-collapse known as Orchestrated Objective Reduction (Orch OR). But the brain is not like a computer. It is noisy, wet and chaotic. So how and where could delicate quantum events occur in the brain?

Penrose and Hameroff focused on the quantum effects in microtubules, the minute lattice structures that make up and network neurones. According to their theory, the surface of these microtubules (which are themselves dipoles) are made up of tubulins or proteins arranged in a hexagonal lattice. It was, and

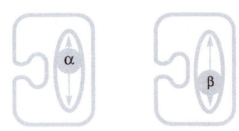

FIGURE 7.6 Quantum superposition in microtubules

maybe still is, their belief that these proteins exist in a quantum state of superposition such that they are simultaneously in both an α and β state. The quantum collapse of these proteins in turn results in a conscious experience, such that a series of collapses leads to a stream of consciousness.

Quantum theory aligns with the phenomenal nature of creative insight. Learning to move into the unknown, to ride waves of vibratory possibilities, is like being in quantum superposition. During the dialogue between the subjective thinker and the creation of the object of thought, meaningful possibilities are infinite, quantumly smeared over space and time. But in the moment of creative insight, this frequency collapses (in this instance not to a flat line) from a possibility into a potentiality.

This is how we make new meaning. It is a moment of repatterning to a higher level of consciousness.

SUMMARY

Evocative leaders are able to create containers and hold spaces because they know how to work with their own *creative* fire, invest in their own *wholeness*, work with the *unknown* and harness these so as to move forward in the world with *elegance* and grace.

They build creative tension and know how to find and follow flow. They bring this all to bear through the quality of their *presencing*, *patterning*, *story-ing* and *de-signing* skills.

Instead of taking up space (with ego, intelligence, fear...), evocative leaders naturally move to the edge of what is known, so they can lean into and co-create the emerging future.

They then pressurize the container by playing with *time*, *space*, *energy* and *information* to tune into waves of vibratory possibilities.

These states and qualities of mind, these subtle skills, and these elements of the implicate order, are all windows into the fourth realm. In this realm evocative leaders open, move and reconnect to the creative rhythms of life, and in turn to the creative rhythms of work. In short, they begin to evoke and call forth the music of innovation.

Evocative leaders then expand this co-creative space so as to enfold others. They create containers and hold spaces in which we can tune into each other's creative rhythms, and leverage each other's talents and contributions. In these co-creative spaces we distribute leadership and allow different people to lead at different times. We are able to build and hold creative tension together; and we collectively hold the space open, ready to find and follow flow.

These containers can be created within existing teams and functions, and they are particularly powerful at new and novel intersections, for this is always where new value always lies.

The challenge of course is how more leaders can learn to step over this post-conventional threshold at will and with skill. And, just as importantly, the challenge is how to teach these subtle skills, in weeks and months, rather than years.

We are against the clock. Time is of the essence if we are to develop a new and next generation of leaders who can help us face into some of the super-wicked problems of our time, and help us shape futures fit for generations to come.

A LIVING EXPERIMENT

Between 1993 and 1996 I had the privilege of being paid as a research associate to undertake doctoral research. Housed between the art and education faculties, my enquiry was into how shifts in consciousness could help us to become more creative. It was a study of methods of self-discovery and their impact on our ability to release our co-creative potential.

It was amazing being paid to meet truly shiny people from creativity specialists to intuition researchers, from mystics to neuro-scientists, from quantum physicists to business leaders... a true mélange of wisdom, all in service of codifying how to design a creative breakthrough – if indeed it was possible at all.

This three-year period was transformational for me. It was an opportunity to weave together different parts of the puzzle – design, emergence, pattern, Zen, consciousness, creativity, creative tension, flow, community – into a coherent whole and into a co-creative methodology.

I discovered that catalysing creative insight is not a linear process, rather it is a layered choreography; and that one of the primary correlates of success is the quality of the 'container' that the designer, artist, catalyst or leader generates first in themselves, and then in turn opens and holds for others.

Before, during and following my PhD I consulted to organizations of all kinds, including many household brands in the UK and all over the world. Through the

Nineties I moved from consulting on design management, to creativity, to visioning, to cultures of innovation. And, in the mid-Nineties I began working as part of a small network of consultants. I remember one important opportunity where we worked together in a particular client for the CEO. Our challenge was to help him turn his business around, against the clock, so it could then be sold for a profit by their parent company. The consulting team included a brand, marketing and strategy specialist, an organizational development (OD) practitioner, a designer, and me. Instead of colluding with the silos of most organizations (brand reporting into marketing, culture into HR, strategy into strategic planning etc) we were given licence to flow through the organization in order to design and deliver a transformational choreography of interventions. The work was successful, and the business was sold for a healthy profit.

After the assignment was complete we debriefed and realized that we had stumbled across something very important. First, we had tapped into the multi-disciplined dimension of our team, enabling us to speak and bridge many functional and commercial languages. Second, we realized that each of us had some kind of personal practice or daily discipline – meditation, running, walking, drawing – that enabled us to slow down, meander, incubate and allow new insights to emerge in the space between.

We were intrigued and excited. Over the next year or so this group morphed into what became the six founders of **nowhere**. It then took two years for this group to design **nowhere** as we were determined to develop a co-creative practice rather than a series of products or offers.

We launched in January 2000 as a trading company and as a not-for-profit foundation. The former was our commercial arm and the latter a place where we could undertake research and apply our emerging practice to education, health and governance. We also chose to be nomadic, with no communal offices.

We've been fortunate in that we've worked (and continue to work) with amazing leaders and companies all over the world. I still pinch myself most days, thrilled with the people, challenges and opportunities that we get to work with.

Just as importantly **nowhere** has remained a living experiment in consciousness, creativity and commerciality.

Personally, **nowhere** has been a creative adventure for me on so many fronts. The most topical of which was being challenged to step forward and become the founding CEO. If you'd asked me at the time, I would have been happy being one of six equals.

So my journey has been one of working alongside some truly inspiring and jaw-droppingly clever leaders, while pursuing my own humble journey of leadership.

EVOKING THE MUSIC OF INNOVATION

Evocative leaders create containers and hold spaces that tune the frequency at which their teams and organizations operate. When this co-creative frequency is reached, cultures of innovation and creative teams seem to manifest like flames.

This is needed now more than ever. A 2011 annual study by Booz and Co, entitled 'Why Culture is Key', outlines how important culture is:

> 'The elements that make up a truly innovative company are many: a focused innovation strategy, a winning overall business strategy, a deep customer insight, great talent, and the right set of capabilities to achieve successful execution. More important than any of these individual elements, however, is the role played by corporate culture – the organization's self-sustaining patterns of behaving, feeling, thinking, and believing – in tying them all together.'

> 'Spending more on R&D won't drive results. The most crucial factors are strategic alignment and a culture that supports innovation.'

There is no doubt that innovation is the key to the future. It has always been thus. It drives economic growth organizationally, regionally, nationally and globally. And yet our approach to innovation continues to be a one-dimensional numbers game.

Innovation is everyone's business. It is not limited to R&D or new product development. It can and should be happening at every level in organizations. Making things better through continuous improvement or discontinuous innovation reconnects us to our shaper/maker instincts and to our desire to build things that have purpose and meaning.

New value creation happens through the development of more innovative products and services, business processes, business models and go-to-market strategies. The conventional approach is to begin with product and service innovation. This is more than reasonable as these are the quickest and most tangible ways of exchanging new value with 'customers'. However, it's easier said than done, and innovation is usually limited to product-line extensions.

A more post-conventional approach is to focus on building cultures of innovation. These intangible containers catalyse innovation at all levels by design.

These containers are created and held by post-conventional leaders who have learned how to evoke the music of innovation. They tune their cultures into co-creative frequencies enabling ecologies of creative teams to ride the highs and lows of the creative process.

TUNING CULTURES

Every organization has a sound. Every organization has a mood. In the same way that you can change an organization's mood,

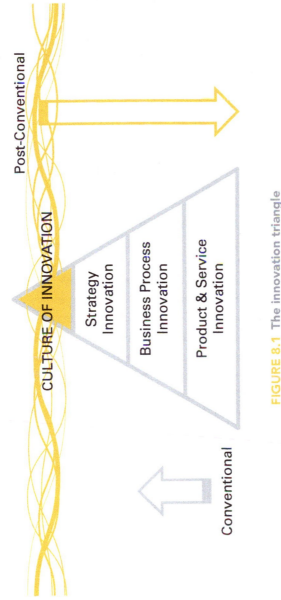

FIGURE 8.1 The innovation triangle

Post-Conventional

CULTURE OF INNOVATION

Strategy Innovation

Business Process Innovation

Product & Service Innovation

Conventional

you can also tune its sound. In tuning its sound, you can transform its form.

This is not a metaphor. I mean this literally.

The art of tuning the frequency of cultures and choreographing pattern shift has a number of pivotal 'dance' steps.

1. Establish core energy

Don't pass go until there is 'core energy'. Core energy is born from leaders who have the authority to shape their system because it is in their gift, ie they don't need to ask for permission from further up the system. They then generate a creative fire, the compelling reason to shift, to leap and to change, while realizing that they too will also need to transform in order to be part of the solution.

From here they build a quorum of post-conventional energy, a small group of colleagues and/or external partners who have the ability to touch into and work from the fourth realm. This core energy is vital for pattern shift, as it is core energy that resources leaders to be bigger than the greatest disturbance in the room or system that they are re-patterning. Without this core energy and identity, leaders struggle to create the necessary tonal container for holding the breakdowns that always precede the breakthroughs.

This core energy is also needed to out-fox the defence mechanisms of organizational systems, as the very issues, blind spots and inherent limitations of the culture will by default get in the way of any intervention intended to interrupt them. It's as if the white blood cells of the host organism come to kill anything that threatens the status quo. This is why core energy is key. It is the wellspring that enables leaders to intentionally disturb themselves and their systems, interrupt defence mechanisms, and move ahead despite their blind spots.

2. Build the leadership container

Evocative leaders use this core energy to attract and develop a wider cadre of leaders to help hold an expanded container. This extended 'federal' team first needs to be on-boarded to each other, and then to the opportunity space, to the nature of the challenge ahead, to the limitations and orthodoxies of current reality and to a new set of skills and ways of working. This is the springboard from which they are then able to participate in, and co-lead, a series of co-creative experiments.

The beauty of this container is that it helps this cadre of senior leaders to develop their 'discovery' skills while still leveraging their existing 'delivery' skills. When they experience the productivity, efficiency and creativity of these leadership containers and spaces (eg new meeting forms), they very quickly go off and scale and replicate them across their own organizational areas.

Building containers is a post-conventional capacity. It is simply not comparable to putting a new tool in your metaphorical backpack. Ultimately it is an energetic phenomenon that takes time to master. The challenge is to help leaders learn about the importance of container building.

For example, we were recently asked to run a series of co-creative experiments with one of our clients. Ultimately they wanted to develop a culture of innovation across their global function, but cautiously chose to experiment first with a number of discrete experiments. We were very clear that these experiments wouldn't add up to pattern shift, while recognizing that each would deliver a business breakthrough in its own right. This approach would give them an opportunity to feel into our practice and for us to learn more about them.

We ran two Breakthrough Projects, three Strategic Landscaping workshops, a Catalyst Training, and a Co-Creative Conference. The last experiment we called 'Building the Leadership Container'. They politely agreed to this last one, giving us the benefit of the doubt. Really they were saying to themselves, 'What's all this mumbo jumbo about containers?'

Three months later we held a review workshop over two days to debrief on each of the experiments. Everyone was delighted with what had been achieved. What was most interesting was how they had moved 180 degrees with regard to their interest in 'container building'. They had learned to see and feel the difference between when they had consciously been holding leadership spaces, and when they had let it slip. This was what most captivated their attention and their desire to take the work to the next level. They could sense the exponential value that they could create once they had learned how to create containers and hold spaces for themselves.

3. Choreograph a sequence of creative interventions

Once leaders have established core energy and built the leadership container, they can start intervening with their organizational system. This is not a developmental intervention, although this is one of the outcomes. Rather it is a set of co-creative interventions designed to generate and accelerate business innovation and breakthrough by catalysing new thinking, relating, learning and organizing with key leaders and their teams. It is this twin dynamic that creates a viral 'pull' from the wider system.

Lighting a creative fire in one place is then followed by lighting a creative fire in another, and so on and so forth. This is how a pattern shift starts to take place. This is when an organization begins to vibrate at a higher, more co-creative frequency, and where leaders become like orchestral conductors.

Like any great orchestral experience, magic happens when the conductor is able to create a container that releases the co-creative potential of the orchestra in ways that also reach out and enfold the audience in a profound, shared experience. These containers create space for everyone's story to be heard, enabling everyone to layer in their own interpretations and thereby create new meaning together.

This is not a critical mass model of change. Rather it is a catalytic model of change, with the leader as catalyst. It only takes a few leaders operating from this place to transform a whole system.

Within this context, tuning cultures is not a soft, HR initiative. It is not a luxury. It should never be seen as on top of the day job. It is the day job, especially for executive and senior leaders.

Culture therefore manifests in the way we do things. To shape more co-creative cultures, we need to shift the way we lead:

- meetings and conferences;
- business-critical projects;
- strategy creation;
- change management;
- the transformation of key functions;
- the development of top talent;
- internal communications;
- branding and design;
- and hothouse innovation.

By focusing on these 'pressure points', we can reprogramme the muscle memory of organizational cultures.

There is a downside. When the container that creates this heightened frequency is no longer held with care and attention, the frequency collapses, and the music stops, or at least becomes less harmonious. Personally, I've seen these containers held at their peak in global corporations for five to six years at a time. When these containers fall away (and this can happen for many reasons), teams and organizations gradually regress to more conventional cultural forms. While a culture may have taken three leaps forwards, without a strong container it will quickly slip back a little.

However, these cultures can be re-enlivened at a later stage, as those co-creative frequencies are now encoded in muscle memory.

4. Invest in infrastructures for growth

In order to resource this choreography evocative leaders also invest in infrastructures for growth. They can do this developing an internal community of change agents to help their leaders and teams step over the threshold into the fourth realm. They also challenge their internal communications teams (who are often unconsciously some of the biggest defenders of the status quo) to step up a level, moving from message-focused to outcome-focused.

Evocative leaders at this stage also seek out the incongruities in their organization's processes and systems that keep their teams and organizations trapped in a conventional, linear and individualist paradigm. For example, the paradigm from which we are measured and incentivized is the paradigm from which we are encouraged to operate, and this needs to align with the new culture.

BUILDING LEADERSHIP CONTAINERS AND DEVELOPING RHYTHM

CHOREOGRAPHING CREATIVE INTERVENTIONS

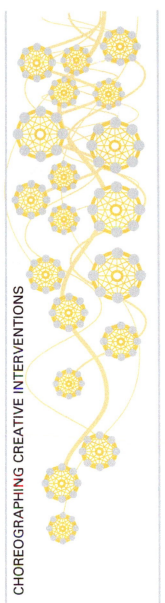

ENABLERS

——— Developing internal catalysts (skills transfer)

——— Developing internal communications capability

FIGURE 8.2 Systemic maps

5. Pay attention to both macro & micro

Evocative leaders also understand that frequency and pattern shift happen by intervening in both the macro and the micro. The challenge at the macro level is to attune collective energy and intent in order to catalyse a new level of meaning and language. This fosters a deeper sense of community, allowing everyone's story to become part of a bigger story.

Meanwhile, the challenge at the micro level is to reshape moment-to-moment interactions. Culture happens in the moment. Without intervening in the way we are with each other, we get stuck in the same old ruts of thinking, relating, learning and organizing. Evocative leaders raise their own self-awareness, as well as the self-awareness of those around them, so as to increase the quality of relationship needed to step into the unknown and sustain not-knowing together. We are then more able to trust, to slow down, to listen that little bit more, to open up that little bit more, so as to maximise the chance of us noticing the fragile shoots of the new.

6. Establish rhythm

Lastly, these ingredients are put together in ways that create and establish rhythm, like a musical score. These rhythms hold teams and organizations on the creative rollercoaster. The team or organization doesn't therefore need an instruction manual, as the force of the ride holds them in place, taking them to new places and spaces.

This is when pattern shift takes place.

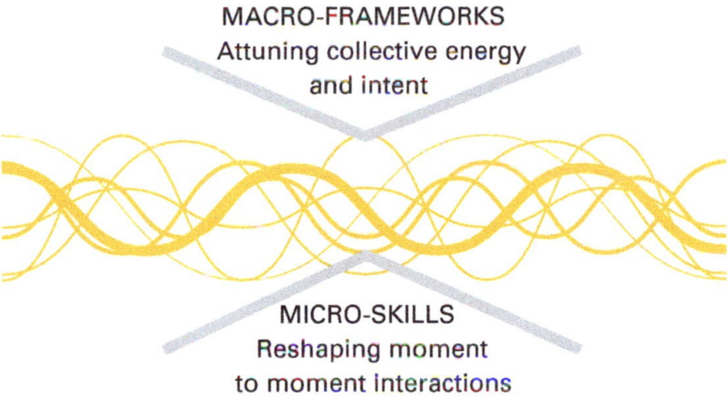

FIGURE 8.3 Macro-frameworks and micro-skills

SUMMARY

At the still point of the turning world.
  Neither flesh nor fleshless;

Neither from nor towards;
  at the still point, there the dance is,

But neither arrest nor movement.
  And do not call it fixity,

Where past and future are gathered.
  Neither movement from nor towards,

Neither ascent nor decline.
  Except for the point, the still point,

There would be no dance,
  and there is only the dance.

– TS Eliot

Conventional leadership has reached a ceiling. The need for a new and next generation of leadership skills is upon us. This next generation of leaders need to know how to design journeys that release our co-creative potential – individually and collectively. And, they need to build organizations and communities and shape futures that we feel proud of being a part of – in business, education, health and government.

To do this they need to understand how innovation is born of co-creative frequencies rather than just the management of rational processes. We of course still need these rational processes but on their own they deny the critical role of the unconscious, invisible, intangible and implicate.

So to complete the circle let's come back to the magic triumvirate and the underlying hypothesis that innovation emerges from co-creative frequencies.

If innovation is about bringing the new into the world, and creativity is about bringing the new to mind, and we can optimize our chance of releasing our creativity by developing particular states and qualities of our consciousness; then leading from the fourth realm is all about tuning ourselves and others into these co-creative frequencies.

These frequencies include: how conscious experience emerges from a stream of quantum collapses, and how creative insight occurs when there is a shift in our alpha and gamma brain waves; how creativity is a dance between the known and the unknown, between our conscious and our unconscious; and how innovation is dependent upon our capacity to work with both the explicate and implicate orders.

Leaders therefore need to learn how to create containers and hold spaces in which we can lean into the implicate order and evoke the music of innovation, at will, with skill, and by design.

To help leaders do this I have outlined some of the subtle skills that I've encountered on my own journey so far. They include:

- using the power of disbelief – 'I didn't know I could do that';
- how creative lows enable creative highs;
- mark-making to allow new patterns to emerge;
- supporting the emotional pain of change;
- calling forth creative fire, wholeness, the unknown and elegant action;
- presencing, patterning, story-ing and de-signing;
- thickening space;
- speeding up and slowing down time;
- playing with energy and information;
- leveraging diversity and difference;

- working with wholeness;
- deepening quality of contact and relationship;
- feeling into the wider context;
- not-knowing;
- tapping into collective intelligence;
- focusing on new and novel intersections (and associations);
- leaning into the space between and to co-create the emerging future;
- embracing creative tension;
- finding and following flow;
- symbols, synchronicity, serendipity, repetition, energy;
- catalysing creative insight and collective breakthrough;
- choreographing the rhythms of change, innovation and transformation;
- elegant execution;
- creating containers and holding spaces that enable all of the above and more.

We are living in exciting and challenging times. We have reached an important threshold. We are already catching glimpses of what lies on the other side. And we are already experiencing what happens to society, and the nature of work if we don't learn to break through into the fourth realm.

The opportunity space is vast. The imperative is nigh. The only burning question left is: Who is ready to step forward?

TABLE 8.1 Old vs new models of leadership

Old models of leadership	New models of leadership
SHIFTS FROM/TO	
Building high-performance achiever cultures	Building cultures of innovation
Controlling linear value chains	Innovating across ecologies of resource
Technology as enabler	Technology as creative catalyst
Silo and matrix structures (mechanical)	Adaptive self-organizing cells (biological)
Planned and objective strategies by numbers	Emergent and subjective strategies by insight
Profit-driven (ie gain)	Purpose-driven (ie contribution)
Baby Boomers/Gen X as the engine room	Gen Y/Millennials as the engine room
The management of change	The choreography of transformation
One-dimensional meetings (operational)	Containers and multiple meeting forms
Innovation managed as a process	Innovation emerges from a co-creative frequency
The linear management of time	Speeding up and slowing down time

TABLE 8.1 Continued

Old models of leadership	New models of leadership
Fact-based decision making	Pattern-based decision making
Competences and capabilities	Capacities and subtle skills
Driving performance (push)	Calling forth/evoking (pull)
Systems thinking (intellectual)	Systemic awareness (phenomenological)
Minimizing tension	Maximizing creative tension
Message-based communication	Outcome-based communication
Ideation-based creative tools	Insight-based collective intelligence
Working with tangibles	Working with intangibles
Learning how to plan work	Learning how to design breakthrough

PERSONAL CODA

It is important to me that this book has been born of practice, not of academic theory. My criteria for success is always, 'Does it work?' What I have shared in this book is what I've seen work, as much as I am pointing to the vanguard of this type of work and the need for this type of work.

What I do know is evoking the music of innovation is a practice. And, as with any good practice, it requires practice. It is with and through practice that we come to connect to a deeper wisdom and tap into the wonders of the implicate order.

Helping leaders, teams and organizations step forward and step over these thresholds is key. The reality is we all need to learn more about what this means and how to do it.

If you would like to join a growing community of fellow questers, please go to: www.now-here.com/community

APPENDIX 1
Riding the creative rollercoaster programme

Riding the Creative Rollercoaster is a three-module intensive training programme that introduces senior leaders to the practice of creating containers and holding spaces in which creativity, productivity and innovation can flourish.

- We explore the secret sauce of designing and catalysing creative insight and collective breakthrough.
- We introduce a new portfolio of frameworks and micro-skills.
- We reveal the hidden patterns that enable or disable change, innovation and transformation.
- And, we invite leaders to step into the fourth realm so they can see how innovation emerges from co-creative frequencies.

Ultimately, this programme introduces the subtle-skills of post-conventional leadership – working with diversity, creative tension, collective intelligence and flow, so as to help teams and organizations embrace the highs and lows of the creative process.

This is what we call riding the creative rollercoaster.

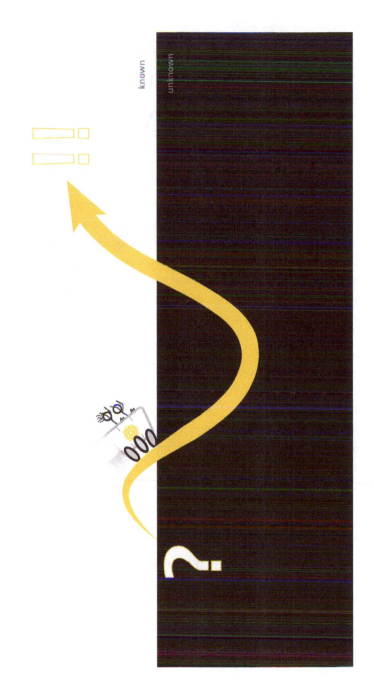

known
unknown

FIGURE A.1 Riding the creative rollercoaster programme

APPENDIX 2
nowheremaps

nowheremaps are reflective and contextual maps that give us insights into: how we can walk through life more co-creatively; how we can lead others more evocatively; how we can unlock the creative potential of important personal relationships and/or critical professional relationships; how we can release the co-creative power of teams and/or the co-creative power between teams; and, how we can tune a culture to be more innovative.

nowheremaps are inspired by an ancient taxonomy of how to live and work co-creatively at the levels of self, other, team and community. Resembling an eight-pointed compass, each direction of the map reveals an ally that releases our co-creative potential and a distortion that diminishes our co-creative potential. We all have these allies and distortions within us. The challenge is how available (at will and with skill) our allies are to us in any given moment, and from moment-to-moment; and how we can learn to see and then interrupt our distorted habits and patterns that get in our way.

By completing the online questionnaire we can map our allied and distorted scores. The greater the volume of our allied map the greater our voltage and our capacity and thereby our ability to ride the highs and lows of the creative rollercoaster.

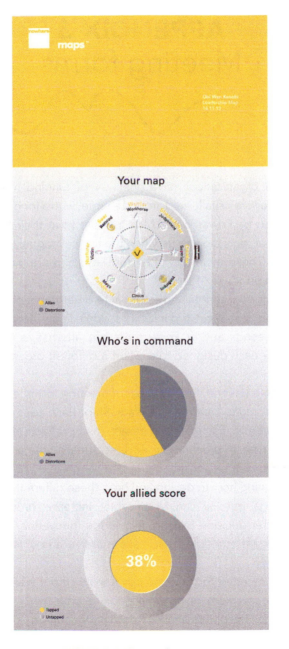

FIGURE A.2 nowheremaps

APPENDIX 3
Meeting forms

Most organizations have one way of running meetings. They are usually held around a table, with a long agenda, and driven by PowerPoints. Most people have their PDAs or laptops out, only looking up when the topic is vaguely relevant to them. These meetings often run late, and are viewed by most as a poor use of time.

Meetings are central and essential to organizational life. The problem is that most organizations don't know how to hold great meetings and/or know there are alternative forms of meeting – each designed to support a different organizational need.

nowhere has codified a number of meeting forms, eg *operational*, *strategic*, *creative* and *leadership*. Each uses information differently. Each has a different rhythm. Each requires a different type of preparation. And, each uses time and space differently.

By learning how to design and hold these different meeting forms organizations can significantly increase productivity, drive better decision making, accelerate innovation, develop more elegant strategies, and save massive amounts of time and energy.

These meeting forms alone can transform our working life, shifting teams from being time poor to time rich – the prerequisite for becoming an innovator/shaper culture.

Operational
meetings
(+)

Strategic
meetings
(x)

Creative
meetings
(x^n)

Leadership
meetings
(**n**)

FIGURE A.3 Meeting forms

APPENDIX 4
Catalyst curriculum

This developmental journey is aimed at change agents and OD professionals who want to learn the practice of catalysis – beyond coaching and facilitation – and become part of a growing and pioneering global community of catalysts.

This multi-levelled curriculum has three key stages. Each stage is made up of three two-day modules. Participants are required to pass each module before they can move onto the next.

TABLE A.1 Catalyst curriculum

Stage 1	Stage 2	Stage 3
Foundational skills	Being the catalyst	The fourth realm
Catalysing meetings	Catalysing new insight	Catalysing strategy
nMaps	Catalysing change	Catalysing innovation

REFERENCES AND FURTHER READING

Anthony, S D (2012) The new corporate garage: where today's most innovative – and world-changing thinking is taking place, *Harvard Business Review* (September)

Atkinson, J (2010) Living systems, adaptive change, in *Total Place: A practitioner's guide to doing things differently*, Leadership Centre for Local Government

Bach, R (1970) *Jonathan Livingston Seagull*, Macmillan

Bateson, G (1972) *Steps to an Ecology of Mind*, Chandler

Benson, R (1991) Learning leadership and the learning organisation, *Visioner & Resultat*, SCF Svenska Civilkonomoforeningen, Sweden, **1**, pp 12–18 and **2**, pp 23–27

Bohm, D (1996) *On Dialogue*, Routledge

Bussey, J (2013) In search of the spark ... and the next big thing, *Wall Street Journal*, 26 March

Carr, A (2010) The most important leadership Quality for CEOs? Creativity, *Fast Company* (May)

Catmul, E (2008) How Pixar fosters collective creativity, *Harvard Business Review*

Cook-Greuter, S R (2005) *Ego Development: Nine levels of increasing embrace*

Csikszentmihalyi, M (1990) *Flow: The Psychology of Optimal Experience*, Harper Perennial

Dyer, F and Gregersen, H (2011) *The Innovator's DNA: Mastering the five skills of disruptive innovators*, Harvard Business Review Press

Edwards, B (1979) *Drawing on the Right Side of the Brain*, HarperCollins.

Getzels, J W (1980) *The Psychology of Creativity*, presented at Carnegie Symposium on Creativity, Inaugural Meeting on the Library of Congress Council of Scholars, 19–20 November

Hamel, G (2012) *What Matters Now: How to win in a world of relentless change, ferocious competition and unstoppable innovation*, Jossey Bass

Hameroff, S (1994) Quantum coherence in microtubules: A neural basis for emergent consciousness?*Journal of Consciousness Studies*, **1** (1)

Harman, W (1990) *Global Mind Change: The promise of the last years of the twentieth century*, Warner Books

Isaacs, W (1999) *Dialogue and the Art of Thinking Together*, Bantam Doubleday Dell Publishing

Jaruzelski, B, Loehr, L and Holman, R (2011) Why culture is key, in *Strategy + Business*, Issue 65 (Winter)

Kiechel, W (2010) *Lords of Strategy: The secret intellectual history of the new corporate world*, HBS Press

Loevinger, J (1998) *Technical Foundations for Measuring Ego Development: The Washington University sentence completion test*, Psychology Press

Maslow, A H (1968) *Towards a Psychology of Being*, Van Nostrand

Owen, H (1990) Learning as transformation (the evolution of consciousness), *In Context*

Penrose, R (1994) Mechanisms, microtubules and the mind, *Journal of Consciousness Studies*, **1** (2)

Ritter, S M, Baaren, R Bvan and Dijksterhuis, A J (2011) Creativity: the role of unconscious processes in idea generation and idea selection, *Thinking Skills and Creativity*, **7** (1), pp 21–27

Rumelt, R (2011) *Good Strategy/Bad Strategy: The difference and why it matters*, Profile Books

Scharmer, O (2009) *Theory U: Learning from the future as it emerges*, Berrett-Koehler

Scharmer, O (2011) *The Future of Change Management: 13 propositions*

Scharmer, O and Kaufer, K (2013) *Leading from the Emerging Future: From ego-system to eco-system economies*, BK Currents

Schwab, K (2012) *Global Agenda Council Summit*, Dubai

Strozzi-Heckler, R and Leider, R (2011) *The Leadership Dojo: Build your foundation as an exemplar leadership*, Frog Books

Torbert, W, Rooke, D and Fisher, D (2000) *Personal and Organisational Transformations: Through action inquiry*, Harthill Group

Udall, N (1996) *The Heuristics of Mindfulness in Higher Art and Design Education*, Roehampton Institute, University of Surrey

Udall, N and Bailey, G (1997) *The Empty Space Drawing Workbook*, **nowhere**

Waitzkin, J (2007) *The Art of Learning: A journey in the pursuit of excellence*, Free Press

Wilber, K (1995) *Sex, Ecology, Spirituality: The spirit of evolution*, Shambhala

Films, tv programmes and podcasts

Horizon, The Creative Brain: How insight works, BBC, March 2013

ABOUT THE AUTHOR

Originally trained in product design, Nick went on to complete a doctorate in Consciousness and Creativity. He has been a breakdancer (a B-Boy), a DJ, a designer, artist, research fellow, teacher and author.

At the age of 23 Nick started to consult to global corporations on visioning, creativity and design management. At the age of 27 he started to design and catalyse business transformations for the CEOs of global corporations, their executive teams and their senior leadership communities.

In 1994 Nick co-founded the Design Transformation Group, a community of international designers, artists, futurologists, educationalists, philosophers and consultants who were interested in shaping the future business of design. And, in the late Nineties, Nick co-founded **nowhere**, as both a community of trading companies and as a not-for-profit foundation.

Today most of his work is with CEOs and their executive and senior teams, designing interventions and transformational journeys. Through this specialist work, Nick has deep-dived into a diverse array of business sectors including: agribusiness, chemicals, pharmaceuticals, energy, banking, FMCG, retail, hi-tech, bio-tech, media and broadcasting, mobile telecommunications, internet companies, the health and beauty industry, manufacturing, high-end engineering, drinks & beverages, and consumer electronics... He has also worked alongside a number of key government departments and agencies.

Nick splits his time between his catalyst work with executive leadership teams, his leadership role in **nowhere**, and sharing his learning and musings in evocative talks.

Nick is also a founding member and the current chair of the World Economic Forum's Global Agenda Council on New Models of Leadership; and is the chairman of The Medicine Garden Cobham, a restored Victorian Walled Garden that won the 2011 Countryside Alliance Award for the South-East of England.

Nick currently lives in Surrey, England, with his wife Caroline, and two children, Kaia and Zen.

www.nickudall.com

ABOUT NOWHERE

Founded in 1998, **nowhere** specializes in releasing the co-creative potential of teams and organizations. Its nomadic community of creative-catalysts travel the world building cultures of innovation and developing breakthrough strategies, through the power of creative teams and evocative leadership.

For further information contact **enquiries@now-here.com** or visit **www.now-here.com**

INDEX